SIMPLE
FABRIC FOLDING for
Halloween

12 Fun Quilts & Projects

Liz Aneloski

C&T PUBLISHING

Text © 2005 Liz Aneloski

Artwork © 2005 C&T Publishing, Inc.

Publisher: Amy Marson

Editorial Director: Gailen Runge

Acquisitions Editor: Jan Grigsby

Editor: Sarah Sacks Dunn

Technical Editors: Franki Kohler and Carolyn Aune

Copyeditor: Wordfirm Inc.

Proofreader: Wordfirm Inc.

Cover Designer/Design Director/Book Designer: Kristy A. Konitzer

Illustrator: Kirstie L. McCormick

Production Assistants: Luke Mulks and Matt Allen

Photography: Luke Mulks and Diane Pedersen, unless otherwise
    noted.

Published by C&T Publishing, Inc., P.O. Box 1456,
    Lafayette, CA 94549.

Front cover: *Spiders Wallhanging* and *Haunted House*

Back cover: *Lollipops on Parade* and *Ghost and Jack-o'-Lanterns*

Library of Congress Cataloging-in-Publication Data

Aneloski, Liz.

  Simple fabric folding for Halloween : 12 fun quilts and projects /
Liz Aneloski.

    p. cm.

  ISBN 1-57120-287-0 (paper trade)

  1. Patchwork—Patterns. 2. Quilting. 3. Origami. 4. Halloween
decorations. I. Title.

  TT835.A49385 2005

  746.46'041—dc22

          2004019319

Printed in Singapore

10 9 8 7 6 5 4 3 2 1

Dedication

To my husband, Mark, who
has supported me every step
of the way. Thank you;
I love you.

Acknowledgments

I would like to thank all of
my friends and co-workers at
C&T Publishing for their
help, support, and fabulous
ideas. My mother, Barbara
Allen, for sewing on a zillion
buttons to help me meet my
deadline, and to Amber and
Ashlyn for their endless
stream of great ideas and
inspiration.

Contents

Double-Folded Triangles

1. Cut a square the size specified in the project instructions.

2. Fold in half horizontally, right sides together, and press.

5. Press.

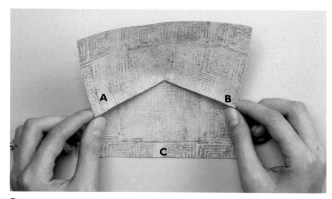

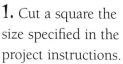

3. Open the square wrong side up. Grasp each end of the crease.

6. Bring the top corner from each side down so the folds meet at the center of the triangle. Press.

4. Bring A and B down to meet at C.

7. Trim.

Pleated Shutters

1. Cut a strip 5½″ × fabric width and trim off selvages. On the right side of the fabric, draw a line 2″ from the end, then 1½″, 1½″, 1½″, 2½″, repeating the pattern to the end of the strip.

2. With wrong sides together, align the first 2 lines and pin. Repeat for the entire length.

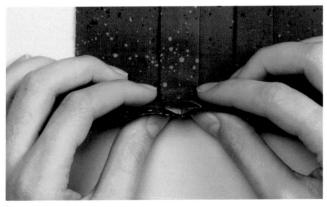

3. Stitch on the marked/pinned lines. Press the pleats flat, centering them over the seamlines.

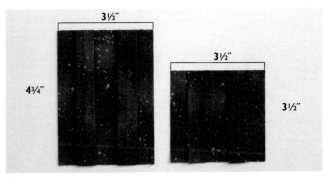

4. Cut shutters apart 3½″ wide, centering the pleats. Trim the longer shutters to 3½″ × 5″ and the shorter shutters to 3½″ × 3½″.

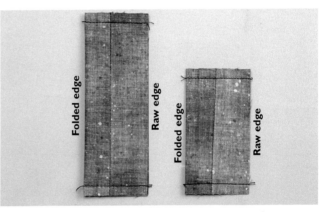

5. Fold in half vertically, right sides together, and stitch along the top and bottom edges, using a ¼″ seam.

6. Turn right side out and press.

Pleated Doors

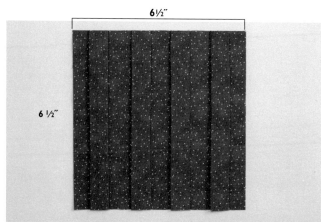

1. Cut a strip 7″ × 16″ and trim selvages. On the right side of the fabric, draw a line 2½″ from the end, then 1½″, 1½″, 1½″, 1½″, 1½″, 1½″, 1½″.

4. Cut the door 6½″ wide, centering the 4 pleats. Trim to 6½″ × 6½″.

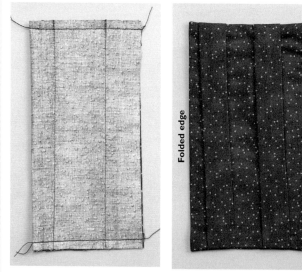

2. With wrong sides together, align the first 2 lines and pin. Repeat for all lines.

5. Fold in half vertically, right sides together, and stitch along the top and bottom edges, using a ¼″ seam.

6. Turn right side out and press.

3. Stitch on the marked/pinned lines. Press the pleats flat, centering them over the seamlines.

Triple-Folded Pentagon Pockets

1. Cut a square the size specified in the project instructions.

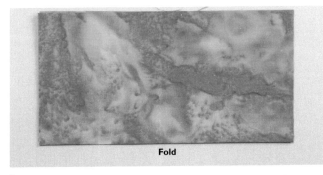

Fold

2. Fold in half horizontally, wrong sides together (with the fold on the bottom), and press.

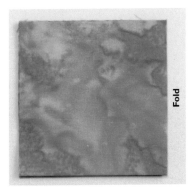

Fold

3. Fold in half vertically (with the fold on the right), and press.

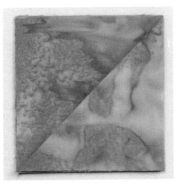

4. Fold the upper left corner down to the lower right corner and press.

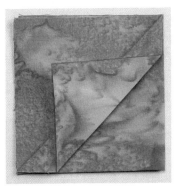

5. Fold the corner back up to create a ½" fold. Press.

6. Tuck the corner behind the fold just created. Press.

(continued)

7. Fold the upper left corner of the second layer to the center.

8. Fold to the center again to create a ½″ fold. Press.

9. Tuck the upper left corner of the third layer to the back, between the third and fourth layers, to create a ½″ fold, and press.

10. Tuck the upper left corner of the fourth layer forward, between the third and fourth layers, to make an edge even with the fold formed in Step 9. Press.

OR

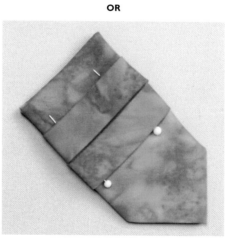

11. Trim or fold as specified in the project instructions.

Folded Fans

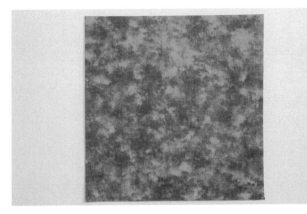

1. Cut a square the size specified in the project instructions.

2. Fold in half horizontally, wrong sides together (with the fold on the bottom). Press.

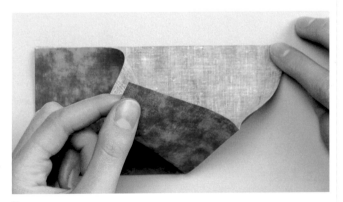

3. Bring the upper right corner to the upper left corner.

4. Adjust the folds to create a triangle in the top layer. Press.

5. Fold the folded upper left corner back to meet the upper right corner.

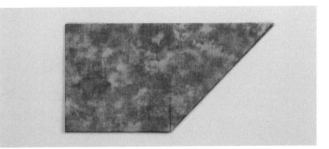

6. Press.

(continued)

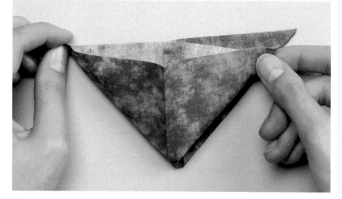

7. Bring the upper left corner to the upper right corner to create a triangle. Press.

8. Trim the raw edges with a wavy-edge rotary cutter blade or wavy-edge scissors.

9. Bring the upper right corner back to the upper left corner and press.

10. Fold in half and press.

11. Fan the layers. Press.

12. Make a second folded fan, and fan the layers in the opposite direction.

Four-Grid Pleated Squares

1. Cut a square of fabric the size specified in the project instructions.

2. Fold the square in half, wrong sides together (with the fold on the bottom), and lightly finger-press.

3. Stitch ½″ (1″) from the fold. (Project instructions specify seam size.)

4. Open the square and press a flat pleat, centering the pleat over the seamline. (See Step 3, page 5.)

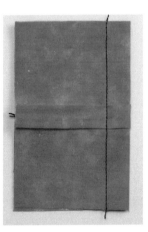

5. Fold the square in half, wrong sides together, and stitch ½″ (1″) from the fold.

6. Press a flat pleat, centering the pleat over the seamline.

Layered, Folded Square-in-a-Squares

1. Cut the squares and rectangles of fabric the sizes specified in the project instructions.

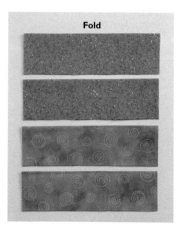

2. Fold the rectangles in half lengthwise, wrong sides together, and press.

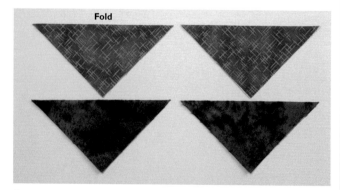

3. Fold the smaller squares in half diagonally, wrong sides together, to make a triangle, and press.

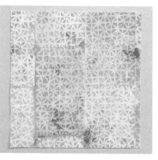

4. Place the large square right side up.

5. Place 2 of the folded rectangles on opposite sides of the large square, matching the raw edges. Then place the 2 remaining folded rectangles on the other 2 sides of the large square.

6. Place 2 of the folded squares (triangles) on opposite corners of the large square on top of the folded rectangles. Then place the 2 remaining folded squares (triangles) on the other 2 corners of the large square on top of the folded rectangles. Alternate the overlapping of the triangle corners as shown. Pin, then machine baste ⅛″ from the edge to secure.

Four-Grid Squares with Prairie Points

1. To make the Prairie Point insert, cut a small square of fabric the size specified in the project instructions.

2. Fold in half diagonally, wrong sides together, and press.

3. Fold in half diagonally in the other direction and press. Set aside.

4. Cut a square of fabric the size specified in the project instructions.

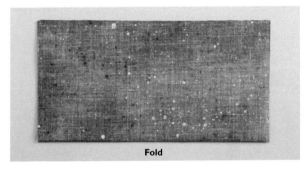

5. Fold the square in half, right sides together (with the fold on the bottom).

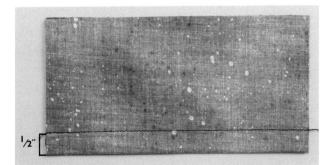

6. Stitch ½" from the fold.

(continued)

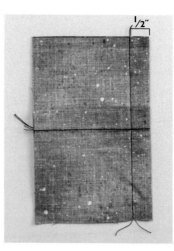

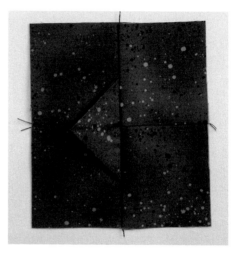

7. Press open.

10. Pin and stitch ½″ from the fold.

8. With the seam of the original square horizontal, fold in half vertically, right sides together.

11. Press open and trim to the size specified in the project instructions.

9. Insert the Prairie Point into the fold, with the tip lined up with the seamline.

Yo-Yos

1. Cut a circle of fabric the size specified in the project instructions and machine baste ⅛″ from the edge.

2. Pull the thread to slightly gather the edge.

3. Turn the edge under ¼″ and press. Tie off the basting threads.

4. Starting on the right side of the circle, hand baste around the circle with perle cotton thread ⅛″ from the edge. Leave a few inches of extra thread. Knot the ends of the thread tails so they will not pull out.

5. Pull the perle cotton thread to gather the circle right side out. *Do not knot the thread,* this will be done during the project construction. Adjust the gathers to form a circle. Depending on the size of the original fabric circle, the center might not close up completely.

Folded Ribbon Chains

1. Cut a piece of ribbon the length specified in the project instructions, and fold it in half.

2. Slide the 2 ribbon layers to form a 90° angle.

3. Fold the piece of ribbon that's the bottom layer up and over to become the top layer.

4. Repeat for the other ribbon layer.

 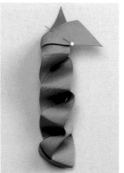

5. Fold alternating sides in this manner over each other until you reach the end of the ribbon. Pin to secure.

Folded Squares
(with eyelet or gathered)

1. Cut a square the size specified in the project instructions.

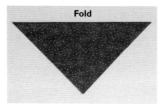 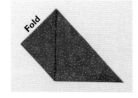

2. Fold in half diagonally, wrong sides together, and press.

3. Bring the left corner down to meet the bottom corner. Press.

4. Bring the right corner down to meet the bottom corner. Press. Machine baste on the 2 raw edges.

Rotate 180° and insert eyelet. **·OR·** *Hand baste with perle cotton thread to gather.*

Options: Insert eyelet, or hand baste with perle cotton thread to gather following the project instructions.

Spooky
WALLHANGINGS

Haunted House

FOLDING TECHNIQUES
Double-Folded
 Triangles
Pleated Shutters
Pleated Doors

QUILT: 36³/₄″ × 39³/₄″

MATERIALS
Yardage is based on 42″ fabric width.
- ½ yard black print #1 for house front
- ⅛ yard black-and-silver stripe for rain gutters
- ⅓ yard black-and-white tiny dot for roofs

- 2 squares 4½″ × 4½″, each of 4 different orange prints for folded roofs
- ⅛ yard each of 8 different Halloween prints for windows and front door
- ⅝ yard purple print #1 for shutters
- ¼ yard purple print #2 for door

(Materials continued)

- ½ yard orange small print for background
- ⅛ yard gray print for porch
- ¼ yard black-and-white check for inner border
- ⅝ yard black print #2 for outer border
- ¼ yard each of 6 different white-and-black prints for folded outer border triangles
- 1¼ yards for backing
- ⅓ yard for binding
- 41″ × 44″ batting
- ¼ yard for hanging sleeve
- 7 clasps (½″ × ¾″) for shutters (see Resources, page 64)
- 3 small (¾″) hinges and 1 medium (1″) hinge for door
- 1 circular charm for door knocker
- Skull confetti
- 8 bat buttons or plastic bats
- 11 jack-o'-lantern buttons (see Resources, page 64)
- Orange #8 perle cotton thread
- Black #8 perle cotton thread

CUTTING

Always remove selvages.

Black print #1

- Cut 2 strips 5″ × fabric width. From this strip, cut in the following order:
  1 strip 5″ × 25¼″ for A.
  5 rectangles 3½″ × 5″ for B.
  2 rectangles 2″ × 5″ for C.
  1 strip 1¼″ × 5″ for D.
  1 strip 4¼″ × 12½″ for E.
  1 strip 2″ × 13¼″ for F.
  1 strip 2″ × 12½″ for G.
  1 strip 2″ × 9½″ for H.

Black-and-silver stripe

- Cut 1 strip 1¼″ × fabric width. From this strip, cut:
  1 strip 1¼″ × 25¼″ for I.
  1 strip 1¼″ × 12½″ for J.

Black-and-white tiny dot

- Cut 1 strip 5″ × fabric width. From this strip, cut:
  3 rectangles 3½″ × 5″ for K.

1 rectangle 3½″ × 5¾″ for L.
1 strip 2¾″ × 13¼″ for M.
1 strip 1¼″ × 13¼″ for N.
1 strip 2¾″ × 12½″ for O.
1 strip 1¼″ × 12½″ for P.

Orange prints

- Cut 2 squares 4½″ × 4½″ from each of the 4 fabrics for Double-Folded Triangles (page 4) to make 8 roofs.

Halloween prints

- Cut:
  1 square 3½″ × 3½″ from 2 of the fabrics for dormer windows.
  1 rectangle 3½″ × 5″ from 5 of the fabrics for house windows.
  1 rectangle 3½″ × 6½″ from 1 fabric for door.
- Cut 4 squares 1¾″ × 1¾″ from 1 fabric for inner border corners.

Purple print #1

- Cut 3 strips 5½″ × fabric width for shutters. Follow the instructions for making Pleated Shutters (page 5). Trim 10 of the shutters to 3½″ × 5″ and 4 of the shutters to 3½″ × 3½″.

Purple print #2

- Cut 1 strip 7″ × 16″ for door. Follow the instructions for making Pleated Doors (page 6).

Orange small print

- Cut:
  3 rectangles 2¾″ × 6½″ for Q.
  1 rectangle 11″ × 13¼″ for R.
  3 strips 1½″ x fabric width for background border. (You will trim to size later.)

Gray print

- Cut 1 strip 1½″ × fabric width for porch. (You will trim to size later.)

Black-and-white check

- Cut 4 strips 1¾″ × fabric width for inner border. (You will trim to size later.)

Black print #2

- Cut 4 strips 4″ × fabric width for outer border. (You will trim to size later.)

White-and-black prints

- Cut 1 strip 5″ × fabric width from each of the 6 fabrics, then cut each strip into 7 squares 5″ × 5″ for the Double-Folded Triangles (page 4) for outer border.

Binding

- Cut 5 strips 2″ × fabric width.

Hanging sleeve

- Cut 1 strip 8″ × fabric width. (You will trim to size later.)

FOLDED UNITS

Make 8 Double-Folded Triangles (page 4) for the roofs.

Make 42 Double-Folded Triangles (page 4) for the border.

Make 14 Pleated Shutters (page 5).

Make 1 Pleated Door (page 6).

CONSTRUCTION

Use ¼″ seam allowance. Press away from the folded units.

Quilt Top

1. Place 2 shutters on top of the corresponding window fabric pieces. Baste ⅛″ from the raw edges of the shutter. Repeat for remaining shutters.

2. Arrange the sections and folded units as shown in the Quilt construction illustration.

3. Stitch the blocks into rows and then sections, inserting the folded units. Press.

4. Place a rectangle Q on the left side of dormer section, right sides together. Stitch at a diagonal. Trim and press. Repeat for the remaining Q pieces.

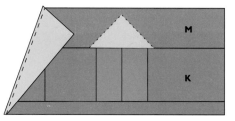

5. Stitch the sections together. Press.

6. Trim the 1½″ gray print strip to 25¼″. Stitch it to the bottom of the quilt top for the porch. Press.

7. Trim 1 of the 1½″ orange small print strips to 25¼″. Stitch it to the top of the quilt top for the background border. Press.

8. Trim the remaining 1½″ orange small print strips to 30¼″. Stitch them to the sides of the quilt top for the background border. Press.

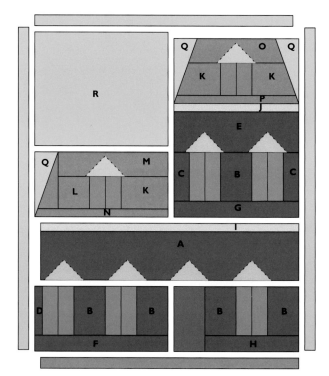

Quilt construction

Borders

Your top should measure 27¼" × 30¼". If it does, follow the instructions below and trim the border strips to the lengths specified. If it doesn't, measure and trim the border strips to fit your top.

1. Trim 2 of the inner border strips to 30¼". Stitch them to the sides of the quilt top. Press.

2. Trim the other 2 inner border strips to 27¼". Stitch an inner border corner to each end of these strips. Press. Stitch them to the top and bottom of the quilt top. Press.

3. Trim 2 of the outer border strips to 32¾". Stitch them to the sides of the quilt top. Press.

4. Trim the other 2 outer border strips to 36¾". Stitch them to the top and bottom of the quilt top. Press.

5. Place 10 overlapping Double-Folded Triangles on the top edge of the quilt top. Baste ⅛" from the edge. Repeat along the bottom edge.

6. Place 11 overlapping Double-Folded Triangles on 1 side edge of the quilt top. Baste ⅛" from the edge. Repeat along the other side.

FINISHING

Quilting

1. Layer and baste (see Quilting Basics, page 61).

2. Stitch in-the-ditch around the blocks.

Finishing Touches

1. Add Double-Fold Straight-Grain Binding (page 62).

2. Add a hanging sleeve (page 63).

3. Be sure to add a label to your Halloween heirloom.

Embellishing

1. With perle cotton thread, hand stitch around the shutters, door, and roofs, taking care to keep them dimensional.

2. Tack pleats on the shutters, as shown in the photo on page 17.

3. Sew on the shutter clasps, door hardware, and knocker.

4. Add the buttons and the skull confetti.

Laundry Day

FOLDING TECHNIQUES

Ghosts (Embellishing, page 24 Step 3)

QUILT: 46½″ × 30½″

MATERIALS

Yardage is based on 42″ fabric width.

- ¾ yard small black print for background, sashing, and binding
- ½ yard orange print for background
- ¼ yard black-and-white print for sashing
- ½ yard Halloween print for border
- 1½ yards for backing
- 50½″ × 34½″ batting
- ½ yard for hanging sleeve
- 2 pieces of cheesecloth 12″ × 12″ (see Resources, page 64)
- 4 small plastic spiders

- 2 plain white handkerchiefs
- Roll of 2″ bandage strips
- Roll of 3″ bandage strips
- Fray sealant
- 2 Styrofoam balls (1″)
- 1½ yards of 6mm rayon cording for clothesline
- 18 clothespins (1″)
- 2 pairs striped doll tights (see Resources, page 64)
- Variety of letters (see Resources, page 64)
- ⅛″ iron-on ribbon for lettering (see Resources, page 64)
- 3 buttons, ⅛″ or 7mm (see Resources, page 64)

CUTTING

Always remove selvages.

Black small print

- Cut 1 strip 6½" x fabric width. From this strip, cut:
2 rectangles 6½" × 10½" for A.
1 rectangle 6½" × 18½" for B.

- Cut 1 strip 1½" x fabric width. From this strip, cut:
2 strips 1½" × 16½" for C.

- 5 strips 2" x fabric width for binding.

Orange print

- Cut 1 strip 16½" x fabric width. From this strip, cut:
2 rectangles 14½" × 16½" for D.
1 rectangle 10½" × 16½" for E.

Black-and-white print

- Cut 3 strips 1½" x fabric width. From these strips, cut:
2 strips 1½" × 6½" for F.
2 strips 1½" × 40½" for G.

Halloween print

- Cut 4 strips 3½" x fabric width for outer border. (You will trim to size later.)

Clothesline cording

- Cut 2 pieces 17".
- Cut 1 piece 13".

Hanging sleeve

- Cut 2 strips 8" x fabric width. (You will trim to size later.)

FOLDED UNITS

Make 2 small ghosts, following Step 3 of the Embellishing instructions (page 24).

CONSTRUCTION

Use ¼" seam allowance. Press toward the sashing and borders.

Quilt Top

1. Use the quilt photo as a guide. Place a cheesecloth square at an angle across an A rectangle. Baste ⅛" from the edge of the fabric on the 2 straight edges of the rectangle. Trim excess cheesecloth. Repeat for the other A rectangle.

2. Arrange the fabric pieces and clothesline cording, as shown.

3. Stitch the sections in rows. Reduce the stitch length as you sew over the clothesline cording. Press.

4. Stitch the rows together. Press.

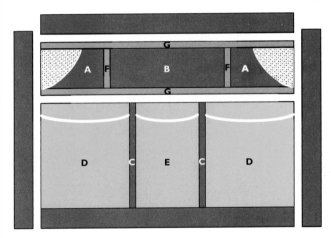

Quilt construction

Borders

Your top should measure 40½" × 24½". If it does, follow the instructions below and trim the border strips to the lengths specified. If it doesn't, measure and trim the border strips to fit your top.

1. Trim 2 of the outer border strips to 40½". Stitch them to the top and bottom. Press.

2. Trim the other 2 outer border strips to 30½". Stitch them to the sides. Press.

FINISHING

1. Trace the lettering as shown on the photo.

2. Trim the excess clothesline cording in the seam allowance to ½″.

Quilting

1. Layer and baste (see Quilting Basics, page 61).

2. Stitch in-the-ditch around the blocks and sashing. Reduce the stitch length as you stitch through the clothesline cording.

3. Stitch diagonal lines through the A rectangles, starting from the outside upper corners, so they look like spiderwebs.

4. Stitch a 2″ grid through the clothesline section.

5. Make a line of stitching in the center of the border, all the way around the quilt.

Finishing Touches

1. Add Double-Fold Straight-Grain Binding (page 62).

2. Add a hanging sleeve (page 63).

3. Be sure to add a label to your Halloween treasure.

Embellishing

1. Fuse and stitch the ribbon to the traced lettering. Dot the I's and complete the exclamation with buttons.

2. Attach the spiders in the spiderwebs.

3. For the ghosts, cut 1 piece of the 3″ bandage strip 4″ long and fold it over the Styrofoam ball. Wrap thread at the ghost's "neck" to secure. Apply the fray sealant to the raw edges. Repeat for the second ghost. Attach the ghosts to the A rectangle by stitching through the "neck".

4. Arrange and sew the letters on the B rectangle.

5. Cut 5 pieces of 2″ bandage strip approximately 9″ long. Apply the fray sealant to the raw edges.

6. Hang the handkerchiefs, tights, and bandages on the clothesline.

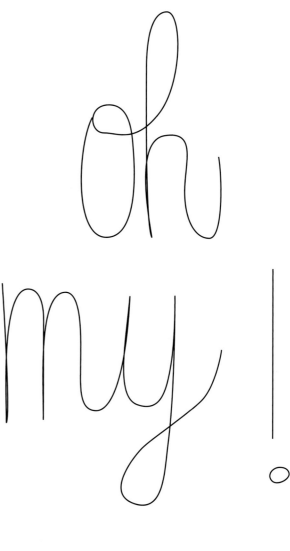

ghosts +
witches
mummies,

Ghost and Jack-o'-Lanterns

FOLDING TECHNIQUES

Triple-Folded Pentagon
Pockets
Folded Fans

QUILT: 41½" × 41½"

MATERIALS

Yardage is based on 42" fabric width.

- 1½ yards Halloween print for background and outer border
- 36" × 36" piece of cheesecloth (see Resources, page 64)
- 1 yard white-on-white print for ghost
- ¼ yard each of 3 different orange prints for jack-o'-lanterns
- ⅝ yard of 36"-wide black felt for jack-o'-lantern accents
- ½ yard black textured print for bats
- ⅝ yard black print for inner border, outer border corners, and binding
- ⅞ yard orange textured print for Triple-Folded Pentagon Pockets for border
- 1¼ yards 17"-wide paper-backed fusible web
- Polyester stuffing for ghost head
- 1⅔ yards for backing
- ¼ yard for hanging sleeve
- 45½" × 45½" batting
- 2 buttons, 1½" or 38mm (see Resources, page 64)
- ¼" masking tape for marking quilting lines

CUTTING

Always remove selvages.

Halloween print

- Cut 1 square 33½″ × 33½″ for background.
- Cut 4 strips 3½″ × fabric width for outer border. (You will trim to size later.)

Note: If you are using directional fabric, cut 2 strips from the horizontal width and 2 strips from the vertical length of the fabric.

White-on-white print

- Cut 1 square 36″ × 36″ for ghost. Cut in half diagonally.
- From 1 triangle, cut 2 circles 5″ in diameter (see pattern, page 50).

Black textured print

- Cut 1 square 10″ × 10″ for Triple-Folded Pentagon pocket for large bat body.
- Cut 2 squares 9½″ × 9½″ for Folded Fans large bat wings.
- Cut 2 squares 1″ × 1″ for large bat ears.
- Cut 3 squares 4″ × 4″ for Triple-Folded Pentagon Pocket small bat body and for Folded Fans for wings.
- Cut 2 squares ¾″ × ¾″ for small bat ears.

Black print

- Cut 4 strips 1½″ × fabric width for inner border. (You will trim to size later.)
- Cut 4 squares 3½″ × 3½″ for outer border corners.
- Cut 5 strips 2″ × fabric width for binding.

Orange textured print

- Cut 3 strips 9½″ × fabric width. From these strips, cut 10 squares 9½″ × 9½″ for Triple-Folded Pentagon Pockets for border.

Hanging sleeve

- Cut 1 strip 8″ × fabric width. (You will trim to size later.)

FOLDED UNITS

Make 12 Triple-Folded Pentagon Pockets (page 7) for the border. Trim the 10 orange pockets to 3½″ wide. Do not trim the black pockets (bat bodies).

Make 4 Folded Fans (page 9) for the bat wings.

CONSTRUCTION

Use ¼″ seam allowance. Press away from the folded units.

Quilt Top

1. Place the cheesecloth on top of the background fabric.

2. Baste ⅛″ from the raw edge around the entire quilt top. Trim excess cheesecloth.

Borders

1. Trim 2 of the inner border strips to 33½″. Stitch them to the sides of the quilt top. Press.

2. Trim the other 2 inner border strips to 35½″. Stitch them to the top and bottom of the quilt top. Press.

3. Trim the 4 outer border strips to 35½″.

4. Evenly space 5 of the folded pockets on 1 of the border strips. Secure the pockets to the border strip by basting ⅛″ from the raw edges. Repeat for another border strip.

5. Stitch these 2 strips to the sides. Press.

6. Add border corner squares to each end of the 2 remaining strips. Stitch the strips to the top and bottom. Press.

FINISHING

Quilting

1. Layer and baste (see Quilting Basics, page 61).

2. Stitch in-the-ditch around the inner border.

3. Using 30°-angle lines, mark and stitch a 3″ grid on the center of the quilt. (Use ¼″ masking tape to mark the grid.)

4. Stitch next to the top and bottom edges of the border pockets.

5. Quilt a zigzag in the top and bottom borders.

Finishing Touches

1. Add Double-Fold Straight-Grain Binding (page 62).

2. Add a hanging sleeve (page 63).

3. Be sure to add a label to your Halloween treasure.

Embellishing

For the jack-o'-lanterns

1. Trace jack-o'-lantern and face shapes onto paper-backed fusible web (see patterns, pages 29–32).

Note: Each jack-o'-lantern has 3 pattern pieces.

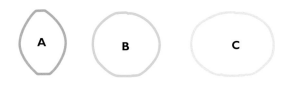

2. Following the manufacturer's directions, fuse the jack-o'-lanterns and the middle eye shape to the appropriate orange fabrics. Fuse the outer and pupil eye shapes, the nose, and the mouth to black felt. Cut out on the traced lines.

3. Fuse the 9 jack-o'-lantern shapes onto the felt, spacing at least ¼″ apart. Layer and fuse the eye shapes, felt, fabric, and felt. Fuse the facial features to the jack-o'-lantern faces.

4. Cut out each of the 9 orange jack-o-lantern shapes, leaving ¹⁄₁₆″ of felt showing around the edges.

For the ghost

1. On the large white triangle for the ghost, turn under ¼″ two times and stitch to finish the 3 raw edges.

2. Place the 2 white circles right sides together. Begin with a backstitch, then stitch around the edge to within 2″ of the beginning stitches. Backstitch. Turn right side out, stuff loosely, and hand or machine stitch to close the opening.

For the bats

1. Fold the sides of the bat bodies and pin as shown.

2. Fold the ¾″ and 1″ squares in half diagonally twice to make the bat ears.

3. Insert the ears into the opening at the top of the bat body and hand stitch in place using invisible stitches.

Insert ears and stitch.

FINAL ASSEMBLY

1. Arrange the pieces (see photo, page 26).

2. Place the stuffed white circle on the quilt background. Center the long edge of the white triangle on the top edge of the stuffed white circle and pin.

3. Hand stitch about 5″ on the curved top edge of the ghost's head to attach it to the quilt top. This allows the ghost to hang freely and makes ironing easy should the ghost get wrinkled.

4. Stitch through the head and quilt to attach button eyes to hold them in place.

5. Position the bats on the quilt top. Pin the wings in place and remove the body. Open the top fold of the wing and stitch in the crease line to secure. Fold back into position. Stitch just below each wing fold.

6. To attach the bat bodies, stitch in the creases next to the folds.

7. Layer A, B, and C sections of each jack-o'-lantern. Stitch through all the layers just around the A sections. This allows the other sections to be dimensional.

Quilt Construction

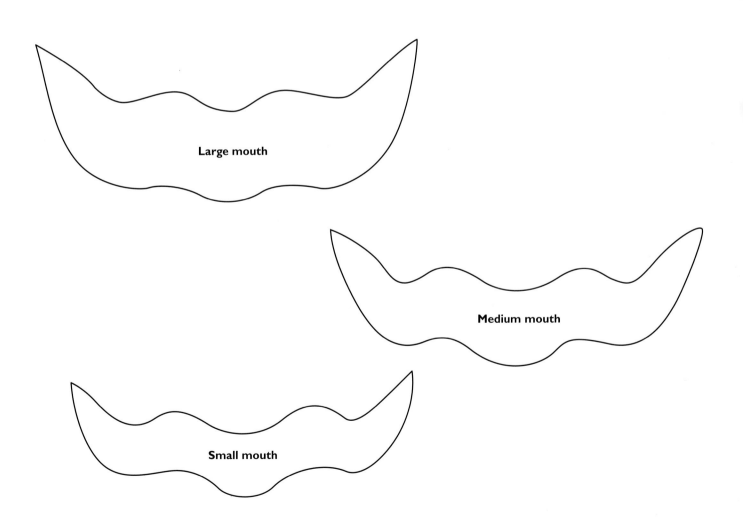

Large mouth

Medium mouth

Small mouth

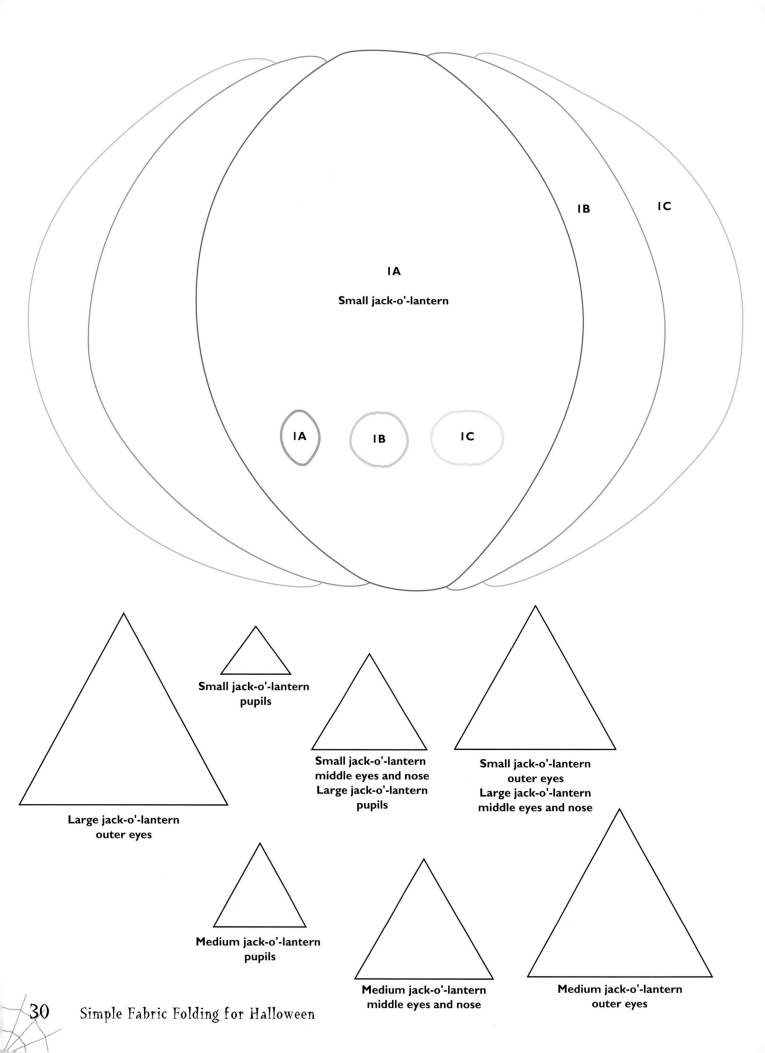

IB

IC

IA

Small jack-o'-lantern

IA

IB

IC

Small jack-o'-lantern pupils

Large jack-o'-lantern outer eyes

**Small jack-o'-lantern middle eyes and nose
Large jack-o'-lantern pupils**

**Small jack-o'-lantern outer eyes
Large jack-o'-lantern middle eyes and nose**

Medium jack-o'-lantern pupils

Medium jack-o'-lantern middle eyes and nose

Medium jack-o'-lantern outer eyes

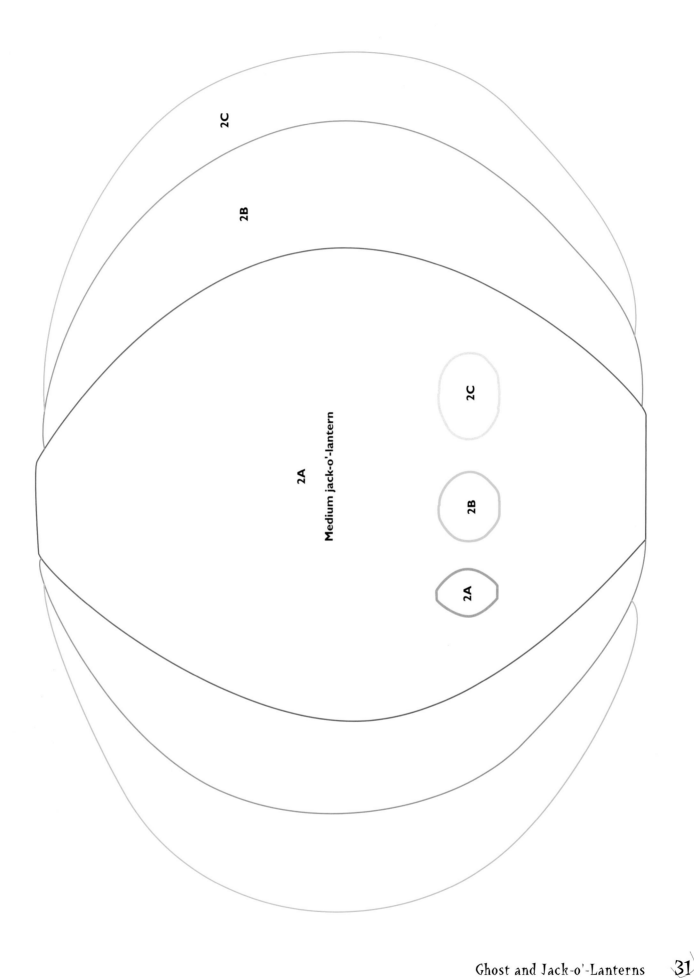

2C

2B

2A
Medium jack-o'-lantern

2C

2B

2A

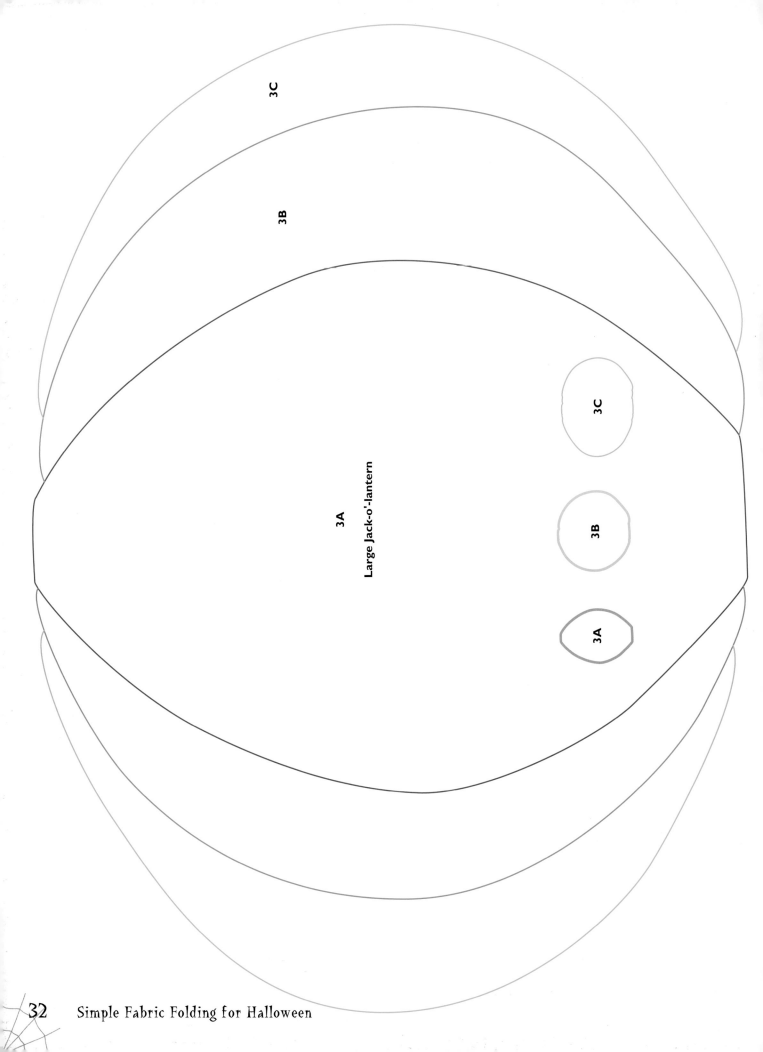

3C

3B

3C

3A
Large Jack-o'-lantern

3B

3A

Simple Fabric Folding for Halloween

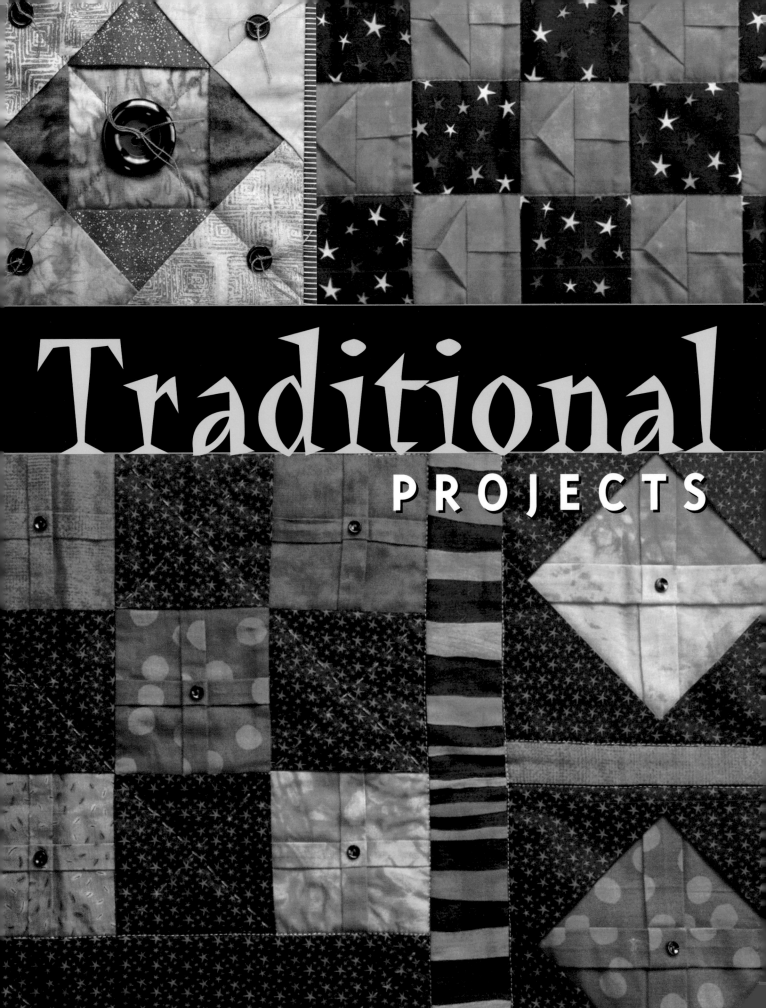

Traditional
PROJECTS

Folded Nine-Patch Wallhanging

FOLDING TECHNIQUES
Four-Grid Pleated Squares

QUILT: 60½″ × 60½″

FINISHED BLOCKS:
6″ and 9″

MATERIALS

Yardage is based on 42″ fabric width.
- ⅞ yard each of 5 orange prints for Nine-Patch blocks, border blocks, and border strips
- 3 yards black print for Nine-Patch blocks, alternate blocks, and border blocks
- ¾ yard black-and-orange stripe for inner border and binding

- 3⅝ yards for backing
- 64½″ × 64½″ batting
- ½ yard for hanging sleeve
- Orange #8 perle cotton thread
- 97 buttons, ⅛″ or 7mm (see Resources, page 64)

CUTTING

Always remove selvages.

Orange prints

- Cut 2 strips 4½″ × fabric width from each of the 5 fabrics (10 total). From these strips, cut 13 squares 4½″ × 4½″ from each fabric for small Four-Grid Pleated Squares (65 total).
- Cut 2 strips 8½″ × fabric width from each of the 5 fabrics (10 total). From these strips, cut: 6 squares 8½″ × 8½″ from 3 of the fabrics for the Four-Grid Pleated Squares (18 total) and 7 squares 8½″ × 8½″ from 2 of the fabrics for the Four-Grid Pleated Squares (14 total).
- From the leftover orange fabrics, cut 32 strips 1¼″ × 6½″ for border strips.

Black print

- Cut 5 strips 3½″ × fabric width. From these strips, cut 52 squares 3½″ × 3½″ for Nine-Patch blocks.
- Cut 3 strips 9½″ × fabric width. From these strips, cut 12 squares 9½″ × 9½″ for alternate blocks.
- Cut 13 strips 4″ × fabric width. From these strips, cut 128 squares 4″ × 4″ for border blocks.

Black-and-orange stripe

- Cut 5 strips 2″ × fabric width for inner border.
- Cut 7 strips 2″ × fabric width for binding.

Hanging sleeve

- Cut 2 strips 8″ × fabric width. (You will trim to size later.)

FOLDED UNITS

Use ½″ stitching to make 65 small Four-Grid Pleated Squares (page 11).

Use 1″ stitching to make 32 large Four-Grid Pleated Squares (page 11).

CONSTRUCTION

Use ¼″ seam allowance. Press away from the folded squares.

Quilt Top

1. Arrange the small Four-Grid Pleated Squares with the 3½″ × 3½″ black print squares.

2. Stitch the squares into blocks. Press. Repeat to make 13 blocks.

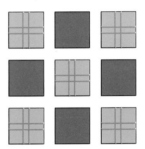

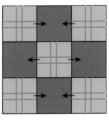

Make 13 blocks.

3. Arrange the Nine-Patch blocks and alternate squares as shown in the Quilt construction diagram (page 36). Stitch the blocks into rows. Press.

4. Stitch the rows together. Press.

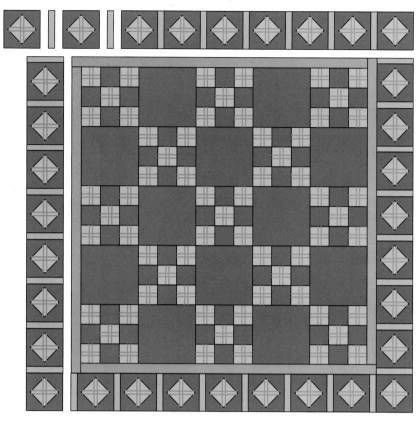

Quilt construction

6. Stitch the blocks and strips for the side borders, then stitch them to the quilt top.

7. Stitch the blocks and strips for the top and bottom borders, then stitch them to the quilt top.

FINISHING

Quilting

1. Layer and baste (see Quilting Basics, page 61).

2. Machine stitch in-the-ditch around the blocks, borders, and border strips.

3. Hand stitch with perle cotton thread, diagonally from corner to corner, through all the black squares.

Borders

Your top should measure 45½″ × 45½″.

1. Remove selvages from the inner border strips. Sew into 1 long strip and cut into 4 strips 2″ × 46½″.

2. Stitch the strips to the 4 sides of the quilt top using the partial seam method (see Quilting Basics, page 61). Press.

3. Fold 4 black 4″ outer border squares in half diagonally with wrong sides together. Press.

4. Place the folded triangles on the 4 corners of a 6″ outer border block, alternating overlapping triangles corners. Baste ⅛″ from the edge to secure. Repeat for the remaining outer border blocks.

5. Arrange the outer border blocks and outer border strips.

Finishing Touches

1. Add Double-Fold Straight-Grain Binding (page 62).

2. Add a hanging sleeve (page 63).

3. Be sure to add a label to your Halloween heirloom.

Embellishing

Stitch a black button to the center of each Four-Grid Pleated Square.

Square-in-a-Square Wallhanging

FOLDING TECHNIQUE
Layered, Folded Square-in-a-Square

QUILT: 36½″ × 38½″

FINISHED BLOCKS
6″, 8″, and 18″

MATERIALS

Yardage is based on 42″ fabric width.

- 3 light orange prints (⅝ yard of 1 fabric, ¼ yard each of 2 other fabrics) for folded blocks and strip sections
- 3 medium orange prints (¼ yard of 1 fabric, ½ yard each of 2 fabrics) for folded blocks and strip sections
- 3 dark orange prints (¼ yard of 1 fabric, ⅜ yard each of 2 fabrics) for folded blocks and strip sections
- ½ yard black print for sashing
- ⅜ yard black-and-white stripe for background and binding
- 1¼ yards for backing
- 40½″ × 42½″ batting
- ¼ yard for hanging sleeve
- Orange #8 perle cotton thread
- 45 buttons (see Resources, page 64):
  - 1 button, 2″ (50mm)
  - 5 buttons, 1¾″ (45mm)
  - 3 buttons, 1½″ (38mm)
  - 4 buttons, 1″
  - 20 buttons, ⅝″
  - 12 buttons, ½″

CUTTING

Always remove selvages.

Orange prints

- Cut 1 square 18½″ × 18½″ from the largest piece of light fabric for the center of the large Folded Square-in-a-Square.
- Cut 4 rectangles 10″ × 18½″, 2 each from the 2 largest pieces of medium fabrics, for the large Folded Square-in-a-Square.
- Cut 4 squares 10″ × 10″, 2 each from the 2 largest pieces of dark fabrics, for the large Folded Square-in-a-Square.
- Cut 5 squares 8½″ × 8½″, 1 each from 5 fabrics (1 light, 2 medium, 2 dark), for the center of the medium Folded Square-in-a-Squares.
- Cut 20 rectangles 5″ × 8½″ (4 light pairs, 4 medium pairs, 2 dark pairs) for the medium Folded Square-in-a-Squares.
- Cut 20 squares 5″ × 5″ (4 light pairs, 2 medium pairs, 4 dark pairs) for the medium Folded Square-in-a-Squares.
- Cut 4 rectangles 2½″ × 8½″, 1 each from 4 fabrics, for the strip sections.
- Cut 3 squares 6½″ × 6½″, 1 each from 3 fabrics (1 light, 1 medium, 1 dark), for the center of the small Folded Square-in-a-Squares.
- Cut 12 rectangles 4″ × 6½″, 2 each from 6 fabrics (2 light pairs, 2 medium pairs, 2 dark pairs), for the small Folded Square-in-a-Squares.
- Cut 12 squares 4″ × 4″, 2 each from 6 fabrics (2 light pairs, 2 medium pairs, 2 dark pairs), for the small Folded Square-in-a-Squares.
- Cut 7 rectangles 2½″ × 6½″, 1 each from 7 fabrics, for the strip sections.

Black print

Note: Cut the longest strips first, then cut the shorter strips from the remaining fabric.

- Cut 5 strips 2½″ × fabric width for sashing. From these strips, cut:
  2 strips 2½″ × 38½″.
  2 strips 2½″ × 18½″.
  4 strips 2½″ × 8½″.
  3 strips 2½″ × 6½″.

Black-and-white stripe

- Cut 2 strips 4½″ × 18½″ for background.
- Cut 4 strips 2″ × fabric width for binding.

Hanging sleeve

- Cut 1 strip 8″ × fabric width. (You will trim to size later.)

FOLDED UNITS

Make 1 large, 5 medium, and 3 small Layered, Folded Square-in-a-Squares (page 12).

CONSTRUCTION

Use ¼″ seam allowance. Press away from the folded squares.

Quilt Top

1. Arrange the blocks, sashing, background, and strip sections.

2. Stitch as shown. Press.

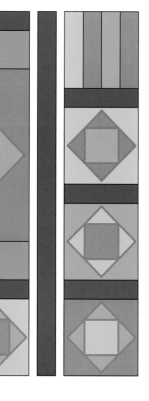

Quilt construction

FINISHING

Quilting

1. Layer and baste (see Quilting Basics, page 61).

2. Stitch in-the-ditch around the blocks, sashing, and strips in the strip sections.

3. To quilt the large square, stitch a horizontal line and a vertical line from the center points of each side of the square. Then stitch 2 diagonal lines from corner to corner to make an X.

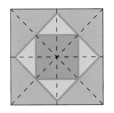

Quilting for large square

4. To quilt the medium squares, stitch 2 diagonal lines from corner to corner to make an X.

Finishing Touches

1. Add Double-Fold Straight-Grain Binding (page 62).

2. Add a hanging sleeve (page 63).

3. Be sure to add a label to your Halloween heirloom.

Embellishing

1. Stitch the 2″, 1¾″, and 1½″ buttons to the centers of the blocks.

2. Stitch the 1″, ⅝″, and ½″ buttons to the corners of the blocks.

Square-in-a-Square Pillow

FOLDING TECHNIQUE
Layered, Folded Square-in-
a-Square

PILLOW: 18″ × 18″

MATERIALS

Yardage is based on 42″ fabric width.

- ⅝ yard light orange print for pillow center and pillow top backing
- ⅓ yard each of 2 medium orange prints
- ⅓ yard each of 2 dark orange prints
- ½ yard complementary orange print for pillow backing

- 20″ × 20″ batting
- 20″ × 20″ pillow form
- 5 buttons (see Resources, page 64):
  1 button, 2″ (50mm)
  4 buttons, 1½″ (38mm)
- Orange #8 perle cotton thread

CUTTING

Always remove selvages.

Orange prints

- Cut 1 square 18½″ × 18½″ from the light fabric for the center.
- Cut 4 rectangles 10″ × 18½″, 2 each from the 2 medium fabrics, for the large Folded Square-in-a-Square.
- Cut 4 squares 10″ × 10″, 2 each from the 2 dark fabrics, for the large Folded Square-in-a-Square.
- Cut 1 square 20″ × 20″ from the light fabric for the pillow top backing.
- Cut 2 rectangles 14″ × 18½″ from the pillow backing fabric.

FOLDED UNIT

Make 1 Layered, Folded Square-in-a-Square (page 12).

CONSTRUCTION

Use ¼″ seam allowance.

Quilting

1. Layer and baste (see Quilting Basics, page 61).

2. Stitch a horizontal line and a vertical line from the center points of each side of the square. Stitch 2 diagonal lines from corner to corner to make an X.

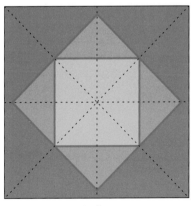

Quilting

3. Trim to 18½″ × 18½″.

Embellishing

Use perle cotton thread to stitch the 2″ button to the center and the 1½″ buttons to the corners.

Pillow Finishing

1. Fold under ¼″ two times on 1 long edge of a pillow backing rectangle. Stitch. Repeat for the other pillow backing rectangle.

2. Place the pillow top right side up. Place the pillow backing rectangles wrong side up, matching the 18½″ sides and overlapping the center. Stitch around the edge.

Place backing on pillow top and stitch.

3. Turn fabric right side out and insert pillow form.

Checkerboard Table Runner and Placemats

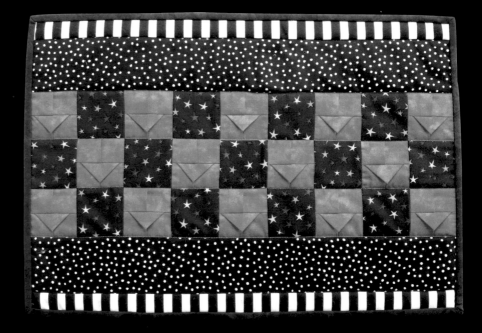

FOLDING TECHNIQUE
Four-Grid Squares With Prairie
 Points

TABLE RUNNER: 12½″ × 54½″

PLACEMAT: 12½″ × 18½″

Note: The instructions are for 1 table runner or 4 placemats. Instructions for placemats appear in parentheses when they differ from table runner instructions.

MATERIALS

Yardage is based on 42″ fabric width.
- ⅓ (⅜) yard black print for checkerboard
- ⅞ (1⅛) yard orange for checkerboard
- ¼ yard black-and-white stripe for narrow border strips
- ⅓ (½) yard black-and-white dot for wide border strips
- 1 yard for backing
- ¼ (½) yard black textured print for binding
- 16½″ × 58½″ (four 16½″ × 22½″) batting

CUTTING

Always remove selvages.

Black print

- Cut 3 (4) strips 2½" × fabric width. From these strips, cut 41 (52) squares 2½" × 2½" for checkerboard.

Orange

- Cut 4 (6) strips 4" × fabric width. From these strips, cut 40 (56) squares 4" × 4" for folded checkerboard squares.
- Cut 3 (4) strips 2½" × fabric width. From these strips, cut 40 (56) squares 2½" × 2½" for simple Prairie Points for folded checkerboard squares.

Black-and-white stripe

- Cut 3 (4) strips 1¼" × fabric width. From these strips, cut 6 (8) strips 1¼" × 18½" for narrow border.

Black-and-white dot

- Cut 3 (4) strips 2¾" × fabric width. From these strips, cut 6 (8) strips 2¾" × 18½" for wide border.

Backing

- Cut in half lengthwise (parallel to the selvages).
- For table runner: With right sides together, stitch into 1 long length.
- For placemats: Cut each piece into 2 pieces, approximately 18" × 21" (4 total).

Black textured print

- Cut 4 (7) strips 2" × fabric width for binding.

FOLDED UNITS

Make 40 (56) Four-Grid Squares with Prairie Points (page 13). Trim to 2½" × 2½".

Note: Be sure to keep the center intersection in the center when you trim.

CONSTRUCTION

Use ¼" seam allowance. Press away from the folded units.

1. Arrange the squares.

2. Stitch the squares into rows. Press.

3. Add the border strips. Press.

FINISHING

Quilting

1. Layer and baste (see Quilting Basics, page 61).

2. Stitch in-the-ditch horizontally between the rows and borders.

Finishing Touches

Add Double-Fold Straight-Grain Binding (page 62).

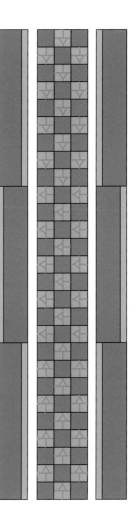

Table runner construction

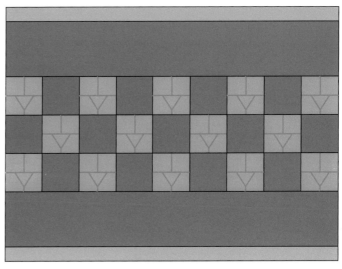

Placemat construction

Creepy DESIGNS

Spiders Wallhanging

FOLDING TECHNIQUES

Yo-Yos

Folded Ribbon Chains

QUILT: 35″ × 35″

MATERIALS

Yardage is based on 42″ fabric width.

- ½ yard black print #1 for background
- ⅞ yard black print #2 for background
- ⅝ yard black print #3 for background
- ½ yard geometric print #1 for large and baby spiders
- ⅓ yard each of geometric prints #2 and #3 for medium and baby spiders
- ¼ yard each of geometric prints #4 and #5 for small and baby spiders
- 1¼ yards for backing
- ⅓ yard for binding
- 39″ × 39″ batting
- ½ yard for hanging sleeves
- Metallic thread
- Black #8 perle cotton thread
- 3 yards ⅜″-wide grosgrain ribbon to match each small spider
- 4 yards ⅜″-wide grosgrain ribbon to match each medium spider
- 5 yards ⅝″-wide grosgrain ribbon to match large spider
- 3 yards decorative cording for baby spiders
- 10 black pony beads (6mm × 9mm) for eye-button shanks
- 10 buttons for eyes (see Resources, page 64):
  2 buttons, 1″
  8 buttons, ¾″
- Template plastic or card stock
- Hot glue

CUTTING

Always remove selvages.

Template plastic or card stock
- Cut 1 circle of each of the following (see patterns, page 50):
  15″, 10″, 7½″, 7″, 5″, 3½″, 2½″.

Black print #1
- Cut one 4″ octagon (see pattern, page 50).
- Cut 2 strips 2″ × fabric width.
- Cut 3 strips 3″ × fabric width.

Black print #2
- Cut 1 strip 2″ × fabric width.
- Cut 3 strips 3″ × fabric width.
- Cut 4 strips 4″ × fabric width.

Black print #3
- Cut 2 strips 2″ × fabric width.
- Cut 4 strips 3″ × fabric width.

Geometric print #1
- Cut 1 circle 15″ in diameter for Yo-Yo large spider (see pattern, page 50).
- Cut 2 circles 2½″ in diameter for Yo-Yo baby spider (see pattern, page 50).

Geometric prints #2 and #3
- Cut 2 circles 10″ in diameter, 1 each from the 2 fabrics, for Yo-Yo medium spiders (see pattern, page 50).
- Cut 4 circles 2½″ in diameter, 2 each from the 2 fabrics, for Yo-Yo baby spiders (see pattern, page 50).

Geometric prints #4 and #5
- Cut 2 circles 7″ in diameter, 1 each from the 2 fabrics, for 2 small spiders (see pattern, page 50).
- Cut 4 circles 2½″ in diameter, 2 each from the 2 fabrics, for 2 baby spiders (see pattern, page 50).

Binding
- Cut 4 strips 2″ × fabric width.

Grosgrain ribbon
- Cut 8 pieces 22″ for large Folded-Ribbon-Chain spider legs.

- Cut 8 pieces for each 15″ medium Folded-Ribbon-Chain spider legs.
- Cut 8 pieces for each 11″ small Folded-Ribbon-Chain spider legs.

Decorative cording
- Cut 20 pieces 5″ for baby spider legs.

Hanging sleeve
- Cut 2 strips 8″ × fabric width. (You will trim to size later.)

FOLDED UNITS

Make 15 Yo-Yos (page 15).

Make 40 Folded Ribbon Chains (page 16).

CONSTRUCTION

Use ¼″ seam allowance.

Piecing the Spiderweb Background

1. With right sides together, place a 2″ black print #2 strip along 1 edge of the octagon. Stitch and press open.

2. Trim both short edges to match the angles of the 2 sides of the octagon.

Place strip on 1 edge of the octagon.   *Stitch and press.*   *Trim.*

3. Working clockwise, place a 2″ black print #2 strip along the second side of the octagon. Stitch and press open.

4. Trim both short edges to match the angles of the 2 sides of the octagon.

Place strip on second side of the octagon.   *Stitch and press.*   *Trim.*

5. Repeat using black print #2 for all 8 sides of the octagon. Trim the last angle parallel to the first sewn side of the octagon.

Repeat for all 8 sides of the octagon.

6. Repeat this process for all of the black print strips, in the following order.

  2″ strips of black print #3
  2″ strips of black print #1
  3″ strips of black print #2
  3″ strips of black print #1
  3″ strips of black print #3
  4″ strips of black print #2

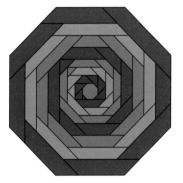

Repeat for all strips.

FINISHING

Quilting

1. Layer and baste (see Quilting Basics, page 61).

2. Use metallic thread to machine quilt in-the-ditch between the octagonal rows.

3. Hand quilt, with metallic thread, to divide the spiderweb into 8 octagonal, pie-shaped sections.

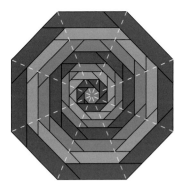

Quilt to divide spiderweb into 8 sections.

Finishing Touches

1. Add Double-Fold Straight-Grain binding, (page 62). Normally, when you come to the corner, you fold up the binding, forming a 45° angle, *which is half the finished 90° angle.* Because this octagon shape doesn't have 90° corners, you will not form 45° angle folds. However, *your fold will still be half the angle of the finished corner.*

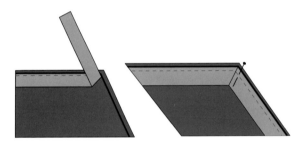

Fold up binding to form a fold half the angle of the finished corner.

2. Make 2 hanging sleeves—1 the length of the top edge of the octagon, and 1 the width of the octagon from side to side (page 63).

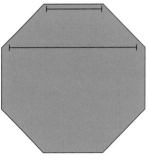

Measure for sleeves.

3. Be sure to add a label to your Halloween treasure.

Spiders Wallhanging   **47**

EMBELLISHING

Making the Baby Spiders

1. Use the 10 smallest Yo-Yos. Knot the thread to secure each Yo-Yo. Trim off the extra thread.

2. Tie a knot in each end of the decorative cording pieces for the legs.

3. Place glue in the center of the flat side of 1 Yo-Yo.

4. Crisscross 4 of the cording pieces on top of the glue.

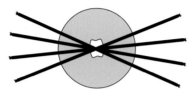

Position cording pieces on glue.

5. Place more glue in the center and add the matching Yo-Yo, sandwiching the legs between the 2 Yo-Yos.

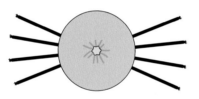

Add matching Yo-Yo.

6. Repeat for all 5 baby spiders.

7. Cut 5 pieces of perle cotton thread 15″.

8. Fold the thread in half and put both ends through the eye of the needle. Insert the needle through the top of the baby spider (through both Yo-Yos). Pull the thread until a small loop of thread forms. Pass the ends of the thread through the loop and pull tight. Remove the needle.

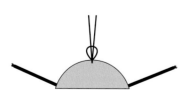

Thread needle, insert into Yo-Yo to form loop, pass needle and thread through loop, and pull tight.

Attaching the Spiders to the Background

1. Open each of the 5 remaining Yo-Yos. Draw a circle on the wrong side of each using the corresponding template: 7½″ for the largest, 5″ for the medium size, and 3½″ for the smallest.

Draw a circle on wrong side of fabric circle.

2. Pull the perle cotton thread to gather the Yo-Yos. *Do not tie off yet.*

Gather the Yo-Yos. Do not tie off yet.

3. Arrange the 5 larger spiders on the spiderweb background and pin in place (see photo on page 45).

4. Position the longest ribbon legs about 1″ under the largest spider body and glue or baste the legs in place under the Yo-Yo. If you glue, be sure the glue is inside the stitching line (the marked line on the wrong side of the fabric circle).

Position legs under Yo-Yo and secure.

5. Open the circle flat and pin around, but not on, the marked circle. Machine stitch on the marked circle.

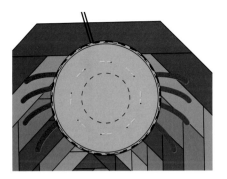

Open Yo-Yo, pin, and stitch.

6. Repeat for all 5 spiders.

7. Pull the perle cotton thread to gather the Yo-Yos. Tie off. Insert the long thread ends into the center of the Yo-Yo.

Gather and tie off.

8. Hand stitch the eye buttons in place, using a pony bead under each button to raise it up out of the Yo-Yo center.

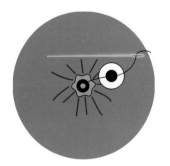

Stitch each button on top of a pony bead.

9. Position and pin the baby spiders on the spider-web background (see photo on page 45).

10. Thread a needle with one end of the perle cotton. Insert the needle into the spiderweb background, and pull the thread to the back.

11. Repeat for the second thread end, inserting it $1/8''$ from the first thread end. Your baby spiders should dangle from web threads 2″–5″ long.

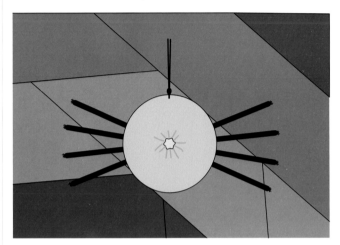

Insert threads $1/8''$ apart.

12. Remove the needle and knot the 2 thread ends at the back of the quilt.

13. Repeat to attach all 5 baby spiders.

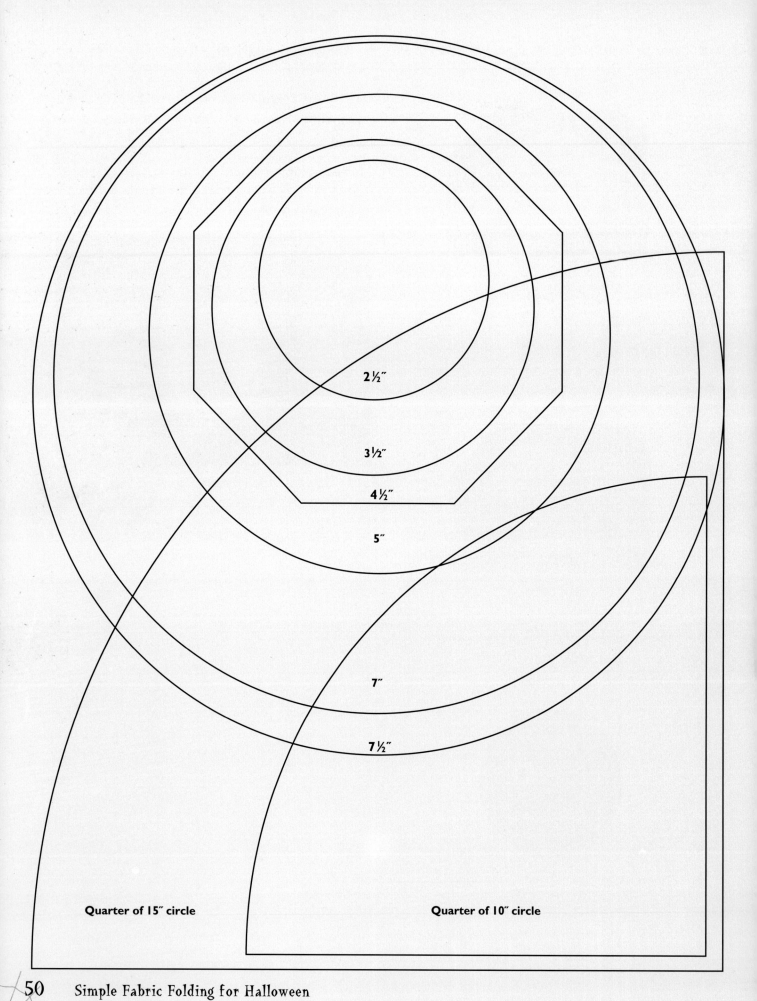

2½″

3½″

4½″

5″

7″

7½″

Quarter of 15″ circle

Quarter of 10″ circle

Spiders Pillow

FOLDING TECHNIQUES
Yo-Yos
Folded Ribbon Chains

PILLOW: 17″ × 17″

MATERIALS

Yardage is based on 42″ fabric width.

- ¼ yard black print #1 for background
- ⅜ yard each of black prints #2 and #3 for background
- ⅓ yard or 1 fat quarter geometric print #1 for medium spider
- ¼ yard each or 1 fat quarter each of 2 different geometric prints #2 and #3 for small spiders
- ¾ yard for pillow top backing and pillow backing
- 21″ × 21″ batting

- 18″ pillow form
- Metallic thread
- 3 yards ⅜″-wide grosgrain ribbon to match each small spider
- 4 yards ⅜″-wide grosgrain ribbon to match medium spider
- 6 black pony beads (6mm × 9mm) for eye-button shanks
- 6 buttons for eyes (see Resources, page 64):
  2 buttons, 1″
  4 buttons, ¾″
- Template plastic or card stock

CUTTING

Always remove selvages.

Template plastic or card stock
- Cut 1 circle of each of the following sizes (see patterns, page 50):
  10″, 7″, 5″, 3½″.

Black print #1
- Cut one 4″ octagon (see pattern, page 50).
- Cut 2 strips 2″ × fabric width.

Black print #2
- Cut 2 strips 2″ × fabric width.
- Cut 2 strips 3″ × fabric width.

Black print #3
- Cut 2 strips 2″ × fabric width.
- Cut 2 squares 7″ × 7″, and then cut in half diagonally.

Geometric print #1
- Cut 1 circle 10″ in diameter for the medium Yo-Yo spider (see pattern, page 50).

Geometric prints #2 and #3
- Cut 2 circles 7″ in diameter, 1 each from the 2 fabrics, for Yo-Yo small spiders (see pattern, page 50).

Grosgrain ribbon
- Cut 8 pieces 15″ for medium Folded-Ribbon-Chain spider legs.
- Cut 8 pieces 11″ for each small Folded-Ribbon-Chain spider legs.

Pillow top backing and pillow backing
- Cut 1 square 21½″ × 21½″ for pillow top backing.
- Cut 2 rectangles 12½″ × 17½″ for pillow backing.

FOLDED UNITS

Make 3 Yo-Yos (page 15).

Make 24 Folded Ribbon Chains (page 16).

CONSTRUCTION

Use ¼″ seam allowance.

Piecing the Spiderweb Background

1. Follow Steps 1–7 (pages 46–47).

2. Repeat this process for all of the black print strips, in the following order.

  2″ strips of black print #3
  2″ strips of black print #1
  3″ strips of black print #2

3. Stitch the oversize triangles to 4 of the octagon sides to form a square. Trim.

Add oversize triangle corners and trim.

FINISHING

Quilting

1. Layer and baste (see Quilting Basics, page 61).

2. Use metallic thread to machine quilt in-the-ditch between the octagonal rows.

3. Hand quilt, with metallic thread, to divide the spiderweb into 8 octagonal, pie-shaped sections (see page 47).

4. Trim to 17½″ × 17½″.

Attaching the Spiders to the Background

Follow Steps 1–8 (pages 48–49).

Pillow Finishing

1. Fold under ¼″ two times on 1 long edge of a pillow backing rectangle. Stitch. Repeat for the other pillow backing rectangle.

2. Place the pillow top right side up. Place the pillow backing rectangles wrong side up, matching the 17½″ sides and overlapping the center. Stitch around the edge.

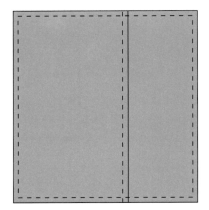

Place backing on pillow top and stitch.

3. Turn the pillow right side out and insert pillow form.

Spiders Countdown Calendar

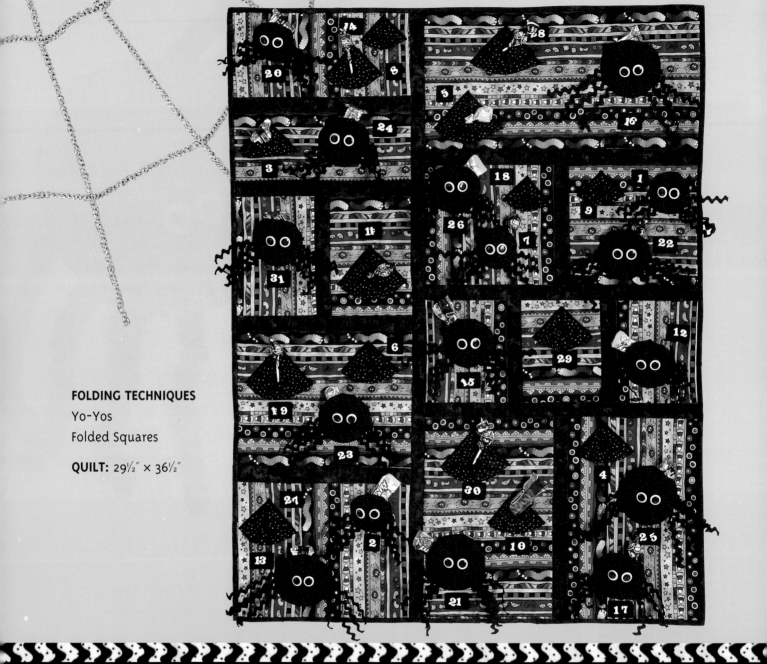

FOLDING TECHNIQUES

Yo-Yos

Folded Squares

QUILT: 29½″ × 36½″

MATERIALS

Yardage is based on 42″ fabric width.

- 1⅛ yards Halloween stripe for background
- ½ yard purple for sashing and binding
- ¾ yard black print #1 for Yo-Yos (spiders)
- ½ yard black print #2 for Folded Squares (pockets)
- 8″ × 10″ black felt
- 1 yard for backing

- 33½″ × 40½″ batting
- ¼ yard for hanging sleeve
- Template plastic or card stock
- Number buttons, 1–31 (see Resources, page 64)
- 32 white buttons, ⅝″ (with a lip around the edge)
- 32 black buttons, ½″ (to fit inside the lip of white buttons)
- 13 yards medium black rickrack
- Black #8 perle cotton thread

CUTTING

Always remove selvages.

Halloween stripe

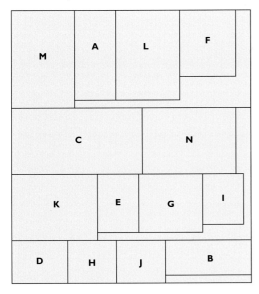

Cutting diagram

■ Cut rectangles (height × width) in the following order, with the stripe running horizontally.

First horizontal section:
   12½″ × 8½″ (M)
   11½″ × 5½″ (A)
   11½″ × 8½″ (L)
   8½″ × 7½″ (F)

Second horizontal section:
   8½″ × 17½″ (C)
   8½″ × 12½″ (N)

Third horizontal section:
   8½″ × 11½″ (K)
   7½″ × 5½″ (E)
   7½″ × 8½″ (G)
   6½″ × 5½″ (I)

Fourth horizontal section:
   5½″ × 7½″ (D)
   5½″ × 6½″ (H)
   5½″ × 6½″ (J)
   4½″ × 11½″ (B)

Purple

■ Cut 5 strips 1½″ × fabric width for sashing. Then cut:
   1½″ × 36″ from strip #1.
   2 strips 1½″ × 17½″ from strip #2.
   1 strip 1½″ × 17½″, 1 strip 1½″ × 6½″, and 1 strip 1½″ × 12½″ from strip #3.
   3 strips 1½″ × 11½″ from strip #4.
   1 strip 1½″ × 11½″, 2 strips 1½″ × 7½″, and 1 strip 1½″ × 6½″ from strip #5.
■ Cut 4 strips 2″ × fabric width for binding.

Template plastic or card stock

■ Cut 1 circle of each of the following (see patterns, page 57.)
   7½″, 6½″, 5½″, 3½″, 3″, 2½″

Black print #1

■ Cut 4 circles with a 7½″ diameter for large Yo-Yo spider pockets (see pattern, page 57).
■ Cut 8 circles with a 6½″ diameter for medium Yo-Yo spider pockets (see pattern, page 57).
■ Cut 4 circles with a 5½″ diameter for small Yo-Yo spider pockets (see pattern, page 57).

Black print #2

■ Cut 1 strip 6″ × fabric width. From this strip, cut 5 squares 6″ × 6″ for large Folded Square.
■ Cut 1 strip 5″ × fabric width. From this strip, cut 7 squares 5″ × 5″ for medium Folded Square.
■ From the leftover fabric, cut 3 squares 4″ × 4″ for small Folded Square.

Black felt

■ Cut 9 squares 1″ × 1″ for backgrounds 1–9.
■ Cut 22 rectangles 1″ × 1½″ for backgrounds 10–31.

Black rickrack

■ Cut 32 pieces 3″ for small spider legs.
■ Cut 64 pieces 3½″ for medium spider legs.
■ Cut 32 pieces 4″ for large spider legs.

Hanging sleeve

■ Cut 1 strip 8″ × fabric width. (You will trim to size later.)

FOLDED UNITS

Make 16 Yo-Yos (page 15), using the template patterns (page 57).

Make 15 Folded Squares (page 16). Beginning at the top corner, use black perle cotton thread to hand baste ¹⁄₁₆″ to ⅛″ from the Folded Square opening edge. Pull to gather, then knot off. These units are now Folded Square Pockets.

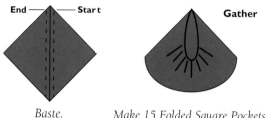

Baste.   Make 15 Folded Square Pockets.

CONSTRUCTION

Use ¼″ seam allowance. Press toward the sashing.

Quilt Top

1. Arrange the blocks. The arrows in the illustration indicate the direction of stripes.

2. Stitch the blocks and sashing into sections. Press.

3. Stitch the sections together. Press.

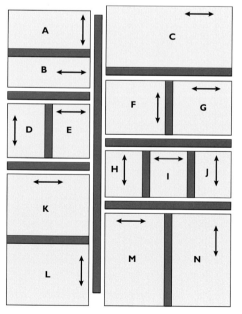

Quilt construction

FINISHING

Quilting

1. Layer and baste (see Quilting Basics, page 61).

2. Stitch in-the-ditch around the blocks.

Finishing Touches

1. Add Double-Fold Straight-Grain binding (page 62).

2. Add a hanging sleeve (page 63).

3. Be sure to add a label to your Halloween heirloom.

Embellishing

1. Arrange the Yo-Yos. Follow Steps 1–4 of Attaching the Spiders to the Background (pages 48–49) to attach the spider pockets. *Note: Leave the top third of the circle unstitched for the pocket opening.*

2. Arrange the Folded Square Pockets. Satin stitch the 2 straight sides to attach.

3. Arrange and stitch the felt number backgrounds (see photo on page 54). Add number buttons.

4. Place black buttons inside white buttons and stitch onto the spiders.

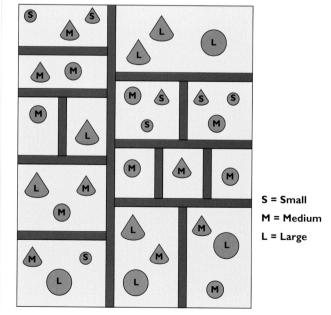

S = Small

M = Medium

L = Large

Pocket arrangement

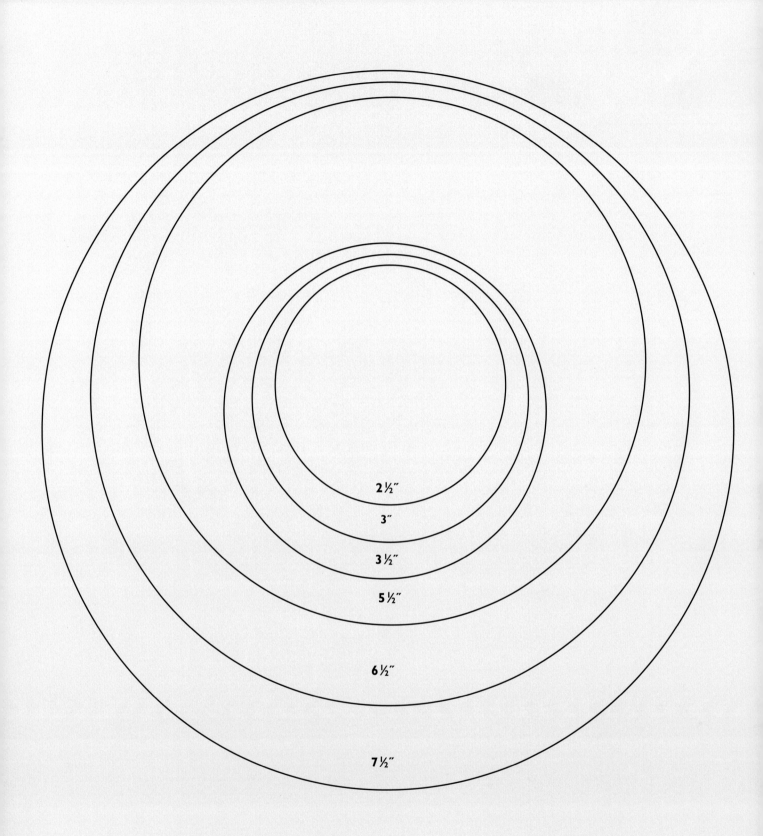

2½″

3″

3½″

5½″

6½″

7½″

Lollipops
on Parade

FOLDING TECHNIQUE
Folded Squares

QUILT: 16″ × 31″

FINISHED BLOCK: 2″ × 2″

MATERIALS

Yardage is based on 42″ fabric width.

- ¾ yards orange print for Folded Square pockets and inset strips
- ¼ yard each or 1 fat quarter each of 6 black prints for background
- ½ yard black textured print for pocket backgrounds and spiderweb background
- ½ yard black-and-gray print for bias binding and hanging sleeve
- 25 eyelets (½″) to hold lollipop sticks
- ⅝ yard for backing
- 20″ × 36″ batting
- 5 yards ⅛″ iron-on ribbon for spiderweb (see Resources, page 64)
- Metallic thread
- 25 small lollipops

CUTTING

Always remove selvages.

Orange print

- Cut 1 square 12″ × 12″ for inset strips.
- From the remaining fabric, cut 25 squares 4½″ × 4½″ for Folded Square pockets.

Black prints

- Cut 12 squares 2¾″ × 2¾″, 2 each from the 6 fabrics. Cut each square in half diagonally in both directions to make 48 side setting triangles (only 46 will be used).
- Cut 2 squares 2⅜″ × 2⅜″, 1 each from 2 fabrics. Cut each square in half diagonally in one direction to make 4 corner triangles.
- From the remaining fabric, cut 2 strips 1½″ x fabric width from each fabric. Cut the strips into squares 1½″ × 1½″ for the background, making 38 squares from each fabric (224 total).

Black textured print

- Cut a half-circle using the spiderweb background pattern (page 60).
- From the remaining fabric, cut 2 strips 2½″ x fabric width. Cut the strips into 25 squares 2½″ × 2½″ for the Folded Square pocket backgrounds.

Black-and-gray print

- Cut 1 square 14″ × 14″ for bias binding (see Continuous Bias Binding, page 62).
- Cut 1 rectangle 8″ × 9″ for hanging sleeve. (You will trim to size later.)

FOLDED UNITS

Make 25 Folded Squares (page 16). Open the fabric and add an eyelet inside the bottom folded corner of each square, following the manufacturer's instructions.

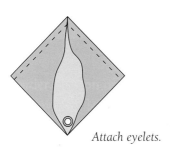

Attach eyelets.

CONSTRUCTION

Use ¼″ seam allowance. Press away from the folded squares.

Quilt Top

1. Arrange the pieces. Be sure to layer the Folded Square pockets on their backgrounds.

Note: Be careful to stitch only 2 sides of the Folded Square pockets onto the background so you can insert the lollipop later.

2. Stitch the pieces into sections. Press.

3. Stitch the sections together. Press.

Stitch sections.

4. Construct a 1″ continuous bias strip from the 12″ square (see Continuous Bias Binding, page 62). Fold the bias strip in half lengthwise, wrong sides together. Press.

5. Cut 2 strips of continuous bias 16″. Set 1 aside. Match the raw edge of the bias strip to the top edge of the quilt top and baste ⅛″ from edge.

Binding

Double-Fold Straight-Grain Binding (French Fold)

1. Trim excess batting and backing from the quilt. If you want a ¼″ finished binding, cut strips 2″ wide and piece them together with a diagonal seam to make a continuous binding strip.

Press.

Sew and Trim.

2. Press the seams open, then press the entire strip in half lengthwise with wrong sides together. With the raw edges even, pin the binding to the edge of the quilt a few inches from the corner, leaving the first few inches of the binding unattached.

3. Start sewing, using a ¼″ seam allowance.

4. Stop ¼″ from the first corner and backstitch 1 stitch. Lift the presser foot and needle. Rotate the quilt one-quarter turn.

Stitch to ¼″ from corner.

5. Fold the binding at a right angle so it extends straight above the quilt.

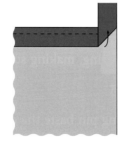

First fold for miter

6. Fold the binding strip down, even with the edge of the quilt.

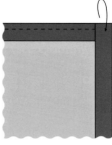

Second fold alignment

7. Begin sewing at the folded edge.

8. Repeat in the same manner at all corners. Proceed to page 63 for Finishing the Binding Ends.

Continuous Bias Binding

1. Cut the fabric square for the bias binding to the size specified in the project instructions. Cut the square in half diagonally, creating 2 triangles.

2. Sew the triangles, right sides together, using a ¼″ seam allowance. Press the seam open.

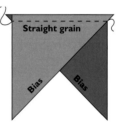

Straight grain

Bias   Bias

3. Using a ruler, mark the parallelogram with lines spaced the width you need to cut your bias binding. Cut about 5″ along the first line.

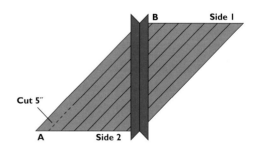

B   Side 1

Cut 5″

A   Side 2

CUTTING

Always remove selvages.

Orange print

- Cut 1 square 12″ × 12″ for inset strips.
- From the remaining fabric, cut 25 squares 4½″ × 4½″ for Folded Square pockets.

Black prints

- Cut 12 squares 2¾″ × 2¾″, 2 each from the 6 fabrics. Cut each square in half diagonally in both directions to make 48 side setting triangles (only 46 will be used).
- Cut 2 squares 2⅜″ × 2⅜″, 1 each from 2 fabrics. Cut each square in half diagonally in one direction to make 4 corner triangles.
- From the remaining fabric, cut 2 strips 1½″ x fabric width from each fabric. Cut the strips into squares 1½″ × 1½″ for the background, making 38 squares from each fabric (224 total).

Black textured print

- Cut a half-circle using the spiderweb background pattern (page 60).
- From the remaining fabric, cut 2 strips 2½″ x fabric width. Cut the strips into 25 squares 2½″ × 2½″ for the Folded Square pocket backgrounds.

Black-and-gray print

- Cut 1 square 14″ × 14″ for bias binding (see Continuous Bias Binding, page 62).
- Cut 1 rectangle 8″ × 9″ for hanging sleeve. (You will trim to size later.)

FOLDED UNITS

Make 25 Folded Squares (page 16). Open the fabric and add an eyelet inside the bottom folded corner of each square, following the manufacturer's instructions.

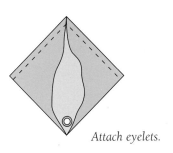

Attach eyelets.

CONSTRUCTION

Use ¼″ seam allowance. Press away from the folded squares.

Quilt Top

1. Arrange the pieces. Be sure to layer the Folded Square pockets on their backgrounds.

Note: Be careful to stitch only 2 sides of the Folded Square pockets onto the background so you can insert the lollipop later.

2. Stitch the pieces into sections. Press.

3. Stitch the sections together. Press.

Stitch sections.

4. Construct a 1″ continuous bias strip from the 12″ square (see Continuous Bias Binding, page 62). Fold the bias strip in half lengthwise, wrong sides together. Press.

5. Cut 2 strips of continuous bias 16″. Set 1 aside. Match the raw edge of the bias strip to the top edge of the quilt top and baste ⅛″ from edge.

6. Fuse iron-on ribbon following the manufacturer's instructions. Use metallic thread to stitch the ribbon to the half-circle (see photo on page 58).

7. Stitch the spiderweb section to the quilt top.

8. Match the raw edge of the bias strip to the bottom left corner of the quilt top, ending at the bottom right corner, and baste ⅛″ from edge. Trim off excess.

9. Baste the remaining 16″ piece of bias strip to the bottom edge of the quilt top, as in Step 5.

Quilt construction and quilting

FINISHING

Quilting

1. Layer and baste (see Quilting Basics, page 61).

2. Stitch horizontally and vertically through the small black squares.

Finishing Touches

1. Add 2″ continuous bias binding (page 62).

2. Add a hanging sleeve (page 63).

3. Be sure to add a label to your Halloween treasure.

Embellishing

Hang small lollipops in the eyelets.

Half of Spiderweb Pattern

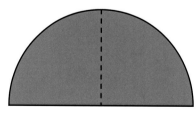

Trace as shown for complete pattern.

Place on fold

Quilting Basics

Fabrics

Fabric requirements are based on a 42″ width. In the cutting instructions, strips are cut on the crosswise grain, unless otherwise noted.

Seam Allowances

Use a $\frac{1}{4}$″ seam allowance.

Pressing

Press the seam allowances away from the folded units. I use steam and moderate pressure when pressing the folded units.

Borders

When cutting border strips on the crosswise grain, diagonally piece the strips together first to achieve the needed lengths. (See Double-Fold Straight-Grain Binding, Step 1, page 62.)

Butted Borders

After you have finished the quilt top, measure it through the center vertically to find the length for cutting the side borders. Place pins at the centers of all four sides of the quilt top, as well as in the center of each side border strip. Pin the side borders to the quilt top first, matching the center pins. Using a $\frac{1}{4}$″ seam allowance, sew the borders to the quilt top and press.

Measure horizontally across the center of the quilt top, including the side borders, to find the length for cutting the top and bottom borders. Repeat pinning, sewing, and pressing, as above.

Partial Seam Borders

1. Place the first border strip on one edge of the quilt top. Stitch partway down the length of the border.

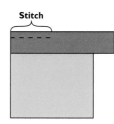
Stitch

2. Stitch the second border to the quilt top. Repeat for the remaining 2 borders. Press.

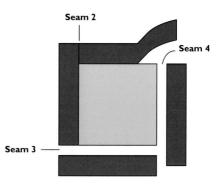
Seam 2
Seam 4
Seam 3

3. Finish stitching the first border. Press.

Backing

Make the backing a minimum of 2″ larger than the quilt top on all sides. Prewash the fabric and trim the selvages before you piece.

Layering

Spread the backing wrong side up and tape down the edges. Center the batting on top, smoothing out any folds. Place the quilt top right side up on top of the batting and backing, making sure it's centered.

Basting

For machine quilting pin baste the quilt layers together with safety pins placed a minimum of 3″–4″ apart. For hand quilting baste the layers together with thread using a long needle and light-colored thread.

Binding

Double-Fold Straight-Grain Binding (French Fold)

1. Trim excess batting and backing from the quilt. If you want a ¼″ finished binding, cut strips 2″ wide and piece them together with a diagonal seam to make a continuous binding strip.

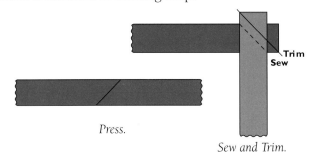

Press.

Trim
Sew

Sew and Trim.

2. Press the seams open, then press the entire strip in half lengthwise with wrong sides together. With the raw edges even, pin the binding to the edge of the quilt a few inches from the corner, leaving the first few inches of the binding unattached.

3. Start sewing, using a ¼″ seam allowance.

4. Stop ¼″ from the first corner and backstitch 1 stitch. Lift the presser foot and needle. Rotate the quilt one-quarter turn.

Stitch to ¼″ from corner.

5. Fold the binding at a right angle so it extends straight above the quilt.

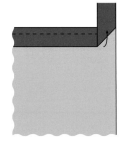

First fold for miter

6. Fold the binding strip down, even with the edge of the quilt.

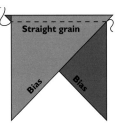

Second fold alignment

7. Begin sewing at the folded edge.

8. Repeat in the same manner at all corners. Proceed to page 63 for Finishing the Binding Ends.

Continuous Bias Binding

1. Cut the fabric square for the bias binding to the size specified in the project instructions. Cut the square in half diagonally, creating 2 triangles.

2. Sew the triangles, right sides together, using a ¼″ seam allowance. Press the seam open.

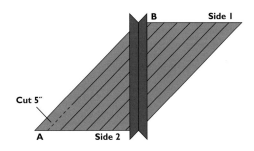

Straight grain
Bias   **Bias**

3. Using a ruler, mark the parallelogram with lines spaced the width you need to cut your bias binding. Cut about 5″ along the first line.

B   Side 1
Cut 5″
A   Side 2

4. Join Side 1 and Side 2 to form a tube. Align A with the raw edge at B so that the first line is offset by 1 strip width. Pin the raw ends together, making sure that the lines match. Sew with a ¼″ seam allowance. Press seams open. Cut along drawn lines, creating one continuous strip.

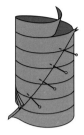

Finishing the Binding Ends

Method 1: Fold under the beginning end of the binding strip ¼″. Lay the end of the binding strip over the beginning folded end. Continue stitching beyond the folded edge. Trim the excess binding. Fold the binding over the raw edges to the quilt back and hand stitch, mitering the corners.

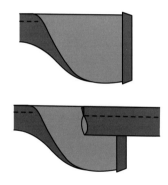

Method 2: Fold the ending tail of the binding back on itself where it meets the beginning binding tail. From the fold, measure and mark the cut width of your binding strip. Cut the ending binding tail to this measurement. For example, if your cut binding is 2¼″ wide, measure 2¼″ from the fold on the ending tail of the binding and cut the binding tail to this length.

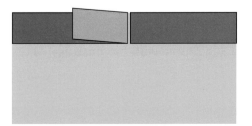

Open both tails. Place one tail on top of the other tail at right angles, right sides together. Mark a diagonal line and stitch on the line. Trim the seam to ¼″. Press open. Fold the binding over the raw edges to the quilt back and hand stitch, mitering the corners.

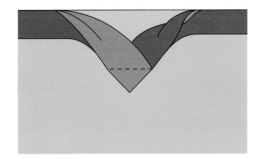

Stitch ends of binding diagonally.

Hanging Sleeve

1. Cut the number of strips indicated in the project instructions 8″ x fabric width. If more than 1 strip is cut, stitch strips together. Press seams open. Measure the top width of the project. Trim the strip to this measurement.

2. Fold ¼″ of 1 short edge. Fold a second time. Press and stitch to finish the edge. Repeat for the other short edge.

3. With wrong sides together, match the 2 long raw edges and stitch.

4. Turn right side out. Press with the seam down the center of one side.

5. Position the sleeve along the top edge of the quilt back and hand stitch. Be sure your stitches do not go all the way through to the front of the quilt.

Resources

SUPPLIES

Folded Nine-Patch Wallhanging
Dill 7mm buttons #150170

Ghost and Jack-o'-Lanterns
Dill 38mm buttons #340001
Dritz 36″-wide cheesecloth

Haunted House
La Mode ½″ × ¾″ clasps #24770
Dill jack-o'-lantern buttons #251271

Laundry Day
Dritz 36″-wide cheesecloth

Necessary Extras
www.necessaryextras.com
Necessary Extras striped doll tights
Making Memories letters
Kreinik ⅛″ iron-on ribbon #6040 cast iron
Dill 7mm buttons #150170

Lollipops on Parade
Kreinik ⅛″ iron-on ribbon #6240 copper kettle

Spiders Countdown Calendar
Dill 11mm number buttons

Spiders Pillow
La Mode 1″ buttons #20465
La Mode ¾″ buttons #20464

Spiders Wallhanging
La Mode 1″ buttons #20465
La Mode ¾″ buttons #20464

Square-in-a-Square Pillow
Dill 50mm buttons #380078
Dill 38mm buttons #340001

Square-in-a-Square Wallhanging
Dill 50mm buttons #380078
Dill 45mm buttons #360002
Dill 38mm buttons #340001

SOURCES

Dill Buttons
www.dill-buttons.com

Dritz
www.dritz.com

Kreinik
www.kreinik.com

La Mode Buttons
www.buttonsplus.com

Making Memories
www.makingmemories.com

About the Author

Liz Aneloski has been quilting since 1981. Her love of quilting began with her first class, which she took as a creative outlet while she stayed home with her two young daughters. The class opened the world of fabric and quilting to her. She especially enjoys trying new techniques that extend just beyond traditional quilting. Liz has been an editor at C&T Publishing since 1991. She lives in California with her husband; her two almost-grown daughters are not far away.

UNDERSTANDING
DIGITAL
PHOTOGRAPHY

UNDERSTANDING
DIGITAL
PHOTOGRAPHY

TECHNIQUES
FOR GETTING
GREAT PICTURES

BRYAN PETERSON

AMPHOTO BOOKS

An imprint of Watson-Guptill Publications
New York

ACKNOWLEDGMENTS

I can't express my gratitude enough to the following people at Amphoto Books: Victoria Craven, Senior Acquisitions Editor; Sharon Kaplan, Editorial and Production Director; Bob Ferro, General Manager; Alisa Palazzo, Senior Development Editor (my ever faithful and talented editor); and designer Bob Fillie. You have all given so much of your time and dedication to my books, and as a result, so many new doors have been opened. Thank you, thank you, thank you again!

And I would also like to pay special thanks to Sharon Lowe, (www.photosbysharon.com) a former student who was the catalyst, in many respects, for my taking on the digital darkroom. Her tips and advice clearly set me down the right path!

Senior Acquisitions Editor: Victoria Craven
Senior Development Editor: Alisa Palazzo
Designer: Bob Fillie, Graphiti Design, Inc.
Production Manager: Hector Campbell

First published in 2005 by Amphoto Books
an imprint of Watson-Guptill Publications
Nielsen Business Media, a division of The Nielsen Company
770 Broadway, New York, NY 10003
www.watsonguptill.com

Typeset in MetaPlusBook and Sabon.

Library of Congress Cataloging-in-Publication Data
Understanding digital photography : techniques for getting
    great pictures / Bryan Peterson.
                            p. cm.
Includes index.
ISBN 0-8174-3796-7 (pbk.)
1. Photography--Digital techniques. I. Title.

TR267.P48 2005
775—dc22
                            2005022321

Printed in the USA

2 3 4 5 6 7 8 9 / 13 12 11 10 09 08 07

To Sophie,
my youngest daughter and fellow shutterbug.
Your enthusiasm for life is always infectious.
You are a gift that I will cherish forever!

Contents

Introduction

Who knows for sure, but someday, the history of photography may be a category on the game show *Jeopardy*, and what a history it is! It all began with the daguerreotype in 1837. In my mind, that episode of *Jeopardy* goes something like this:

"I'll take History of Photography for $200 please, Alex."

"This was the first "fixed" photographic image."

"What is the daguerreotype?"

But back to reality: Although the daguerreotype exposure time was long by today's standards (a bit under thirty minutes), this was, indeed, the first "fixed" image that *did not* fade. This was a true milestone for photography, and needless to say, the world was about to change. Everyone would soon be "traveling" to places and events without ever leaving the confines of home. And although it sounds like an eternity by today's standards, it wasn't until 1884, forty-seven years later, that George Eastman invented flexible paper-based photographic film and another four years after that, in 1888, that he patented the Kodak roll-film camera.

But leave it to the good Reverend Hannibal Goodwin, who a year later in 1889, invented celluloid photographic film. His invention was so good that George Eastman started to make celluloid film, but Eastman was soon slapped with a lawsuit for patent infringement by Goodwin. This legal battle, which began in 1902, wasn't resolved until 1912! (I guess the road to winning lawsuits today is not much faster than it was back then.)

Once his legal battles were behind him, the good Reverend was about to go into the film business when he was, apparently, killed in a "street accident" near a construction site. If not for his untimely death, many of us might have grown up on an advertising slogan such as "Take winning photos with good film—Goodwin film, that is!"

It would be only two years later when the first 35mm still camera was developed (in 1914), but it would be another twenty-one years before the world saw the first roll of Kodachrome slide film (in 1935) and another six years (1941) before the world saw Kodacolor color print film. This was just in time for World War II, but the cost of developing and printing color images was still more than the newspapers and many magazines could afford, and this accounts for all the black-and-white photographs we see from that era.

Shortly after the war, in 1947, the first instant black-and-white camera was invented by Polaroid. With the ending of the war, boyfriends married their girlfriends and husbands

were reunited with their wives. It was a festive time, and I'm sure the immediacy of results with this new, instant camera was enjoyed by many of these couples. Although it didn't offer the best picture quality, was only black and white, and the images would show signs of fading over time, it was meant to entertain—as well as to be a camera for those who couldn't wait to get their pictures developed.

In 1970, the first truly instant color camera came on the market, from none other than Polaroid: the Polaroid SX-70. It was no mess, no fuss, just press the button and out pops the color print—and within a minute or two you have your image, which was permanent, too! This was the best thing in instant photography to date, but it wasn't until 1990 when Kodak, following years of research, unveiled the first Photo CD as a storage medium and soon after, in 1991 to be exact, Kodak teamed with Nikon to create the first digital still camera, using the Nikon F-3 body equipped with a 1.3 megapixel sensor.

Fast-forward to the year 2005 and photography now finds itself at the center of more attention and fascination than perhaps in any other time in history. And of course, it's all about the ever-changing—and thus, at times, confusing—world of digital photography. Never before has such a tiny screen (the LCD) caused such a stir of emotions. No sooner than you fire the shutter release, then everyone gathers around the back of the digital camera to see the results. Expressions of joy or shouts of frustration fill the air quickly as the digital camera lives up to its promise of instant gratification—even if that promise includes the not-so-gratifying evidence that something went terribly wrong!

If there is one prevailing digital-photography mantra being shouted from the rooftops by camera owners worldwide, it is this: "I don't ever to have buy film again! I can shoot and shoot and shoot, make tons of mistakes, and never worry about going overboard on my film costs—that's why I love digital!" So, is conventional photography as we know it dead? Listening to the industry watchers, the consensus seems to be no, at least according to the likes of Fuji and Kodak. The "match" between film shooters (or those who have now become "the purists") and those who have given it all up for digital has just begun. I understand the purist mentality. I once was a purist myself. And, although we are still in the early days, digital photography has already impressed both the judges and fans at ringside. Digital photography is truly a formidable opponent to those purists, and I for one believe that the day will come when digital will finally deliver the knockout blow.

It was just a little over a year ago when I was called by *Popular Photography* magazine to "get into the ring" representing the film shooters for a story called, simply, "Film versus Digital." Being the film purist I was, I gladly took the job and couldn't wait to start sparring. I would be going head to

head with Mike McNamara, the digital editor at *Popular Photography*, and the readers would see for themselves who the "winner" was. Based on reader mail, it can be argued that this bout ended in a draw, but it wasn't long after this match that I found myself struggling with my "valid" reasons for not going digital. Soon, I was embracing digital as a real and viable medium for image-making. The punches that Mike McNamara threw had a lasting impression on me.

Over the past six months, shooting digitally is *all* I have done, and I see a limited use—and I want to stress *limited* use—for the more than 220 rolls of E-100VS I have still sitting in my freezer. Other than the occasional client who wants both film and digital, and for the occasional time exposure beyond 15 seconds, I am now 100 percent digital!

I, like so many other seasoned professionals, am starting over in many respects. It has been a formidable task, as I have had so much to learn; but with that has come a reawakening of my early years when I first held a camera in my hand. Back then, each and every day was one of wonder, amazement, and challenge, and that same childlike feeling is again upon me today. I can't read enough about what's hot, nor can I wait to try this or that. To borrow a worn-out phrase, "I am like a kid in a candy store!"

But, as every parent knows, that kid needs to use some caution. The speed at which digital photography has roared onto the scene would make even Jeff Gordon take notice. This week's hot item is soon replaced by another that can do it even faster and with even greater efficiency. I would be foolish to write a book about many of these must-have items of today; many of these "hot" items will have become dinosaurs before this book even goes to press. If you're looking for advice on what's hot and what's not, buy the most current digital photography magazine, because you won't find that stuff here.

However, despite the rapid pace of digital technology, there still remain *two* constants in the world of image-making. And I doubt if these two constants will ever really change, at least not in my lifetime: Almost since day one, 99 percent of all *successful* photographic images have relied on the photographer's knowledge, skill, and talent (1) in setting a creatively correct exposure and (2) in creating a well-balanced and compelling composition. These things apply regardless of whether you shoot film or digital.

Getting a correct exposure has never been easier than it is with today's digital cameras, but there's often a vast difference between a correct exposure and a creatively correct exposure. This book will show you the difference between the two, but I want to stress that this is not a book that focuses 100 percent on exposure. (I've already written that book—twice, in fact, with its new revised edition—and it's called *Understanding Exposure*.) This book will help you "see" and

also learn how to avoid the most common pitfalls faced by so many digital photographers. The number one problem that shows up in digital images today is the same problem that shows up in traditional film images: ineffective composition.

A lack of attention to what is really going on in the viewfinder is the primary reason why compositions fail. If you never really paid attention to what was going on in your film camera's viewfinder, do you honestly think you'll do any better with a digital camera? Some shooters obviously do think this, since the LCD screen is one of the primary reasons they're drawn to digital photography. As one of my students said to me recently, "I love my new digital camera. When I make a mistake, I can see it on the camera's monitor and then, hopefully, correct it right away; but if not, I can do it later with Photoshop."

Yikes! This is exactly what I'm talking about. What is it about that little itsy-bitsy monitor that is more revealing than the camera's own viewfinder? I had one student tell me she loved her digital camera so much because her monitor was in color! "Because it's in color!?" I said with an expression of disbelief. "And when you look through the viewfinder of your digital camera, do you see black and white!?" And then it occurred to me what was really being said: The monitor makes the image real—it makes it believable, it brings it to life. Sound familiar?

One of the threads that runs through this entire book is this: It's not so much about what we *see*, but rather what we *don't see*, that impacts the success of our images. This book will teach you, in a fresh and exciting way, how to avoid many of the common visual traps into which photographers are prone to fall.

I am, of course, familiar with the enthusiastic refrain "I'll just fix that in Photoshop!" I hear it with reckless abandon during the first few weeks of my online photo courses, but I'm pleased to say that by the seventh or eighth week I hardly hear it at all.

Please don't misinterpret me here, either. I fully appreciate the enthusiasm about Photoshop. I love it just as much as anyone, and I've found it to be an amazing tool; but for so many shooters, Photoshop has become the auto-body shop where photographers take their damaged and wrecked images for repair. Why show up at the doorstep of Photoshop with damaged goods? Sure Photoshop can fix a lot of stuff, but without your creative input, your camera or Photoshop won't be able to do much for you. Most of the damage is caused by nothing else than a lack of attention to what was going inside your camera's viewfinder.

Correcting that problem in camera is so much quicker. So, this book is filled with examples on how to get it right in camera so that when you finally show up at the doorstep of

Photoshop, you are ready to take these same images to the next level—and with Photoshop, that could prove to be an infinite level. But since I'm a strong believer in getting it right in camera, you'll see where I've made numerous references to the dos and don'ts when it comes to the Photoshop "tools" at your disposal. For example, it is possible to render a busy background as an indistinguishable blur with Photoshop, but it might take you upward of twenty minutes to do that. Why would you want to do that when you can learn how to do it *in camera* in less than 1/125 sec.?

I've also included a number of ideas to get your adrenaline pumping, and as you'll see, you don't have to travel far to create compelling imagery—there's a wealth of subject matter to shoot right in your own home as well as on the street in front of you. And you certainly have nothing to lose by trying.

Remember, digital "film" is free (give or take a few memory cards)! The digital camera has not only become the means to make compelling imagery, but with its instant feedback via the LCD monitor, it has also become, in many respects, the teacher, too!

ALL THAT
DIGITAL "STUFF"

WHAT'S A PIXEL?

asked my youngest daughter the other day a perhaps silly question, but I was curious what her answer might be. "If you had a doll named Pixel, would she be smaller or bigger than other dolls?"

She thought about it only for a few seconds and replied, "Definitely smaller than the other dolls, but who would name a doll Pixel anyway?"

"No one has, as of yet," I replied, "but that's the name of those remarkably itsy-bitsy teeny-weeny sensors inside my digital camera, and they're responsible for making the many pictures I've taken of you this past year."

"Yeah, whatever," she replied as she went off to her bedroom to watch a DVD.

Of course she had no idea that the movie she was about to watch was also made possible because of pixels. In what has quickly become the digital age, anything digital—from cameras to iPods to DVDs to CDs—relies on pixels. Pixels are like this huge "family" that, photographically speaking, is at the core of every recorded image. In effect, the pixels are information gatherers, and they are responsible for every digital image ever made. (The word *pixel* is derived from the words picture and element.)

Pixels "live" in a house called the *image sensor*. And the moment you press the shutter release on your camera, light streams through the lens and the Pixel family goes to work gathering information from that light. In a mere fraction of a second an image is recorded. And just a second or two later, the Pixel family has sent this information to your memory card (storage device), making it available for your viewing pleasure on your camera's LCD monitor.

Every digital camera has a family of pixels working for it, but not all families are the same size. In some cameras the Pixel family is three million strong, in others it's five million,

while in still others it's six, seven, eight, and, as of this writing, twelve and sixteen million strong. When it comes to pixels, size does matter, and you'll understand why in a minute, but suffice it to say, the more pixels the merrier.

Each and every pixel is a microscopic square or hexagon, depending on the camera manufacturer, and each has a pre-assigned "seat" within the confines of its home (again, the image sensor). Each one of these squares responds to that very minute portion of light that strikes it, and like one big happy family, all of the pixels—at the same time—perform a very complex mathematical calculation of these light waves, which are then converted into an image by the on-board image processor. On a strictly individual level, each pixel cannot record an image of anything that you or I would recognize as the photograph we just took. Quite the contrary, the Pixel family relies on each and every family member to do the one job it has been assigned, and then collectively the family delivers the finished goods to the image processor.

(This sounds a bit like socialism, doesn't it? If Stalin or Mao Tse-tung were alive today, perhaps we would see their ideals turned into digital cameras instead of tragic and failed attempts at making "digital people.")

And one more thought about pixels: If I had a net with half-inch openings in the weave and you had a net with three-inch openings in the weave, and we both cast our nets into the ocean, who would catch more fish, both big and small? Obviously, I would. In photographic terms, the "fish" we're all hoping to catch translate into color, contrast, and sharpness, so it only stands to reason that the bigger one's Pixel family, the larger the "catch." Eight million pixels are capable of gathering up far more sharpness, contrast, and color than four million—regardless of whether you shoot in JPEG, TIFF, or raw mode.

Pixels are information gatherers, and they are responsible for every digital image ever made.

Two images but, wow, what a difference in over all color and quality. One was taken with a 3.2-megapixel camera (opposite, top); the other with an 8-megapixel camera (opposite, bottom). Note the difference in color, sharpness, and contrast. Clearly, the more pixels you have, the more detail you will capture.

Both photos: 50mm focal length, ISO 100, f/16 for 1/125 sec.

THE THREE DIGITAL IMAGE FORMATS

Digital imaging offers you the choice of processing your image into one of three formats, or types of electronic files. The format you choose will affect not only the immediate outcome of an image's detail, clarity, contrast, and color, but also its long-term stability.

These formats are referred to as follows: JPEG (Joint Photographic Experts Group), TIFF (Tagged Image File Format), and raw (which isn't an acronym—it literally means *raw* as in "raw meat"). It's important to understand that all three formats are assigned a specific file size, meaning that the processed image is made of X number of megabytes—for example, 1.4 megabytes or 5.7 megabytes or 17 megabytes.

So, after you take a digital image, say, of your son that's made up of six million pixels, that picture information is sent to the camera's image processor. It is then processed as a JPEG or TIFF file, or if you've chosen the raw format, it won't be processed at all, but rather stored in a buffer for processing later. (As of this writing, many camera brands offered the three file format choices mentioned above. Canon, however, recently announced that they were dropping the TIFF option since they found that most users of their DSLR (digital single-lens reflex) cameras shot in either JPEG or raw mode. So don't be surprised if you discover that the likes of Nikon, Minolta, and Pentax will soon follow suit.)

It's also important to understand that all three of these formats generate a unique file size that's determined by the format. JPEG is a small file, raw is a medium file, and TIFF is a large file.

The number of files you can store on a memory card will vary depending on which camera you own, but on average, you can store about three to four times as many JPEGs versus raw files and five to six times as many versus TIFFs. For example, with a 1-gigabyte card in a 6-megapixel camera, you can expect to shoot about 424 images in JPEG FINE mode, 124 in raw mode, and 59 in TIFF mode.

JPEG: LOSSY OR LOUSY?

As I mention in the box to the right, due to smaller file sizes, many photographers love to shoot in JPEG FINE, but what many shooters don't realize is this: JPEG files are what are referred to as *lossy* files, or what I like to call *lousy* files. As I've already witnessed firsthand, calling a JPEG a lousy file has stirred up more than one hornet's nest, but hear me out and then you can decide for yourself if JPEG is indeed a lousy or a good choice for you.

The scientific term "lossy" is derived from the word *loss*, as in *to lose*, and it refers to a JPEG file's inability to hold and maintain the original data (the actual image) over time. Every time you open and close a JPEG file on your computer, the file degrades due to data being lost; and eventually, with repeated openings and closings, the file would be rendered useless. In effect, the JPEG can't remember who it is, where it's at, how it got there, or where it's going.

For this reason, every camera manual, digital photography book, and digital photography magazine recommends the same thing that I'm about to recommend: If you insist on shooting in JPEG format, and if you care at all about the "life expectancy" of your images, then after you have carefully chosen which JPEGs are truly keepers you *must* save each and every one of them as TIFF files using your photo software program. (More about TIFFs in a minute.)

Despite this solution of converting JPEGs to TIFFs, there is still some more bad news to consider when shooting in the JPEG format. In a nutshell, due to what is called *compression*, a JPEG image is akin to listening to your favorite rock, rap, or country music on AM radio. Rather than capturing every tiny detail of color and contrast in a scene, the JPEG format takes a shortcut and averages out the "like" colors and the "like" contrast, and then it squeezes the data like a sponge—or compresses it—so that it becomes a tiny file. Just as you lose a lot of the high-end treble and low-end bass on AM radio, you lose a lot of the subtleties in the color spectrum with JPEGs.

Even after you save a JPEG as a TIFF, you're making a permanent save of a file that is still missing some of the "treble" and some of the "bass." Granted, now that it's a TIFF, you will be able to "hear" it in stereo, but it will "sound" like it's being played through some bad speakers.

As far as I'm concerned, the *only* time .jpg should be your image file extension is when you're planning to share the photos with family and friends via the Internet.

TIFF

Although the TIFF is an acronym for Tagged Image File Format, I think of TIFF

A NOTE ABOUT JPEGS

Only the JPEG format offers three types of "profiles": JPEG FINE, JPEG NORMAL, and JPEG BASIC. By default, most digital cameras are set up to shoot JPEG FINE, since this is the highest-quality JPEG possible. And since JPEG produces the smallest image file, it remains a popular choice with many photographers—since each image takes up less space in the memory card (see page 20). Less space per image on the memory card translates into more images per memory card, and for many shooters, that's reason enough to shoot in JPEG FINE mode.

---

as This Is Final Forever! TIFF is the permanent seal of protection! Once a TIFF, always a TIFF—no matter how many times you open the file, no matter how many copies you make of the file, no matter how many alterations you make to the file in Photoshop, it will always remain, at its core, a TIFF. And unlike the JPEG, with its lossy format, TIFF will pick up every last detail and color in your scene, and it has the memory of an elephant: It will never degrade or lose data.

Not surprisingly, just like an elephant, TIFFs generate the biggest file size. Camera type determines just how big the files are, but the size can range anywhere from 17 megabytes to over 60 megabytes. Yikes! With file sizes like that you will burn through a 512 MB memory card in nothing flat.

But it's not the file size that should concern you or cause you to steer clear of choosing the TIFF format for your shooting; there's a better reason: permanence. Remember, my TIFF acronym is This Is Final *Forever*, with the emphasis on *forever*. Once you shoot an image in TIFF format, you cannot alter its exposure at its core *without* spending some extensive time in Photoshop—and that's assuming that the "bad" exposure you're trying to alter is just a minimally bad exposure, i.e. your highlights are a bit blown out or your shadows are a bit too dark.

Furthermore, all digital images are exposed using the principle of white balance (see page 26), and in TIFF format, just like in JPEG, you can't change the white balance once the image is recorded without once again spending needless time in Photoshop making the necessary color corrections.

So, what's the solution if you want to shoot images that have a relatively small file size and capture all the details with no loss of data? In addition, is there also a solution that will correct your "bad" exposure or your white balance at the press of a button before the image is processed? Yes. The answer is the raw format.

RAW MODE

Imagine for a moment that the year is 1990, and you are at the park with your family using a film camera. You've just finished shooting a brand new type of 36-exposure color slide film. This new slide film allows you to take the film out of the camera, remove it from its cassette, and unfurl it in broad daylight so that you can actually see the results before taking the film to the lab for permanent processing. With careful inspection, you notice that eleven of the thirty-six shots you took are off in their exposure by a stop or two. Then there are those other three shots that you now know, as a result of your review, would look better in black and white.

No problem. You simply take out the special marker that came with the film, put an X on each of the bad exposures, mark the other three images as black and white, and reload the film into its cassette. The next day, you drop the film lab, tell them your markings, and sure enough, when you return after work to pick up the film, every shot is just the way you wanted. If you believe this story, then as the saying goes, I have a bridge to sell you, too. Of course, it's not true and never will be if you're a film shooter; but if you're shooting *digitally* and if you're using the raw format, then this story is true!

As I said before on page 18, the word *raw* is not an acronym for anything. But since I obviously cannot live in a world without creating my own acronyms, I came up with one: Really Amazing Work. If you want the best possible exposure, the best possible color, and the best possible contrast in your photos, then raw is for you.

TIP PROCESS YOUR RAW FILES IN 16-BIT MODE

Most of us do make corrections—minor as they may be—to our digital raw files in post-processing. When processing your raw files, you should do so in 16-bit mode. In 8-bit mode, you have 256 levels (or what are called *shades*) per channel (red, green, *and* blue). In 16-bit mode, you have over 65,000 levels (shades) in each channel! And, with Photoshop CS, you can make corrections in 16-bit mode while using Layers. Accessing the Filter menu, however, is a different story. You must convert to 8-bit mode before the Filter palette becomes available. Converting to 8-bit mode is a snap: Just go to the Image pulldown menu, choose Mode, and select 8 Bits/Channel.

Along the same lines of getting the biggest color bang for your buck, it makes no sense to do all your raw processing if the color space of your monitor is set to sRGB. The folks at Photoshop continue to make sRGB the default color space. sRGB is a color space designed for "Web colors," which is another way of saying "color is not that important." But color is important, especially when processing raw files. So, if you haven't already done so, press Shift + Command + K (for Macs) or Shift + Control + K (for PCs) to call up the Color Settings dialog box. Click on Working Spaces and choose Adobe RGB 1998. Don't change this setting unless you hear of a new color space that's even better (which, in all likelihood, will happen one day).

With raw, you can change your exposure up to two stops in either direction—darker or lighter. With raw, you can change the white balance, color temperature, or with some software editing programs, you can even convert the image from color to black and white or sepia, all while the image remains in its raw state. After you're done making minor (or major) adjustments to the image, you can then choose Save As, select TIFF as your file type, and permanently save those changes. And, since you used the Save As command, the original raw files remains the same.

So, to recap and since I feel that most of you are resigned already to shooting in either JPEG or raw, think of the differences between the two this way: JPEG is prepared meat loaf; it has the basic ingredients that will allow you to simply go home, put it in the oven, and have a decent but uneventful meal forty-five minutes later. Raw, on the other hand, is raw meat with all of the necessary ingredients and spices at your disposal. How you prepare the raw meat, and what you add or don't add, is completely up to you. You are the chef, and even with limited cooking knowledge, you can learn the skills and soon place a meal to remember in front of your family and friends.

As friends, colleagues, and all of my students will attest, I despise the on-camera flash. Not only do I hate the artificial look of the light, but even more so, I don't have a clue how to use one with any degree of consistency. I can light up a factory with huge studio strobes or light a model for a fashion shoot, but I'd rather have toothpicks shoved under my fingernails than suffer the pain and anxiety of trying to get results with an on-camera flash.

Several months ago when my daughter Sophie's class had an art show, I showed up with my D2X and fired off a few proud frames without a flash. If there ever were a reason to embrace digital, it's for its ability to let you change to a higher ISO at the turn of a wheel, and also to switch the white balance in post-processing. The first image (opposite, top) is my normal Cloudy +3 white balance setting, which, when combined with the room's tungsten light, accounts for the unusually "warm" look and the excessive red/yellow cast. Not a problem, since once I loaded the image into Photoshop, I simply changed the white balance to Incandescent/Tungsten and the image was corrected (opposite, bottom).

Both photos: 17–55mm lens

DIGITAL "FILM": THE MEMORY CARD

Imagine walking into a casino in Las Vegas and purchasing a prepaid gambling card for one hundred dollars. You are then free to walk up to any dollar slot machine, put the card in, and play that machine a minimum of 125 times. I say *minimum* because this is a magic card that lets you "erase" every spin that doesn't have a payoff and credit your card with another turn. But wait, it gets even better. After you've used up all 125 spins from this card, the casino's computer downloads your winnings and, presto, just like that the card is returned to you with another 125 spins *free of charge*! Welcome to the world of digital "film."

Film, as we knew it, is no longer an issue. The constant lament of film being too expensive or of waiting for the film to be developed is now in the past. The digital photographer has to buy but one "roll of film," and that's it! And what is this one "roll of film"? A *memory card*. Memory cards are the digital media to which your exposures are saved as you make them.

Using a 1 megabyte (MB) memory card and a 6 megapixel camera as an example, that one "roll of film" can result in 428 exposures if you shoot in JPEG FINE, or 130 exposures if you shoot in raw, or 54 exposures if you shoot in TIFF. And, just like the prepaid slot machine card, a memory card can be renewed (i.e., reused) over and over and over. But wait, there's still more good news! That same card will record images at any number of ISOs, and depending on the camera, you can shoot some images at ISO 125, others at ISO 200 or 400, and still others at ISO 1000. Try that with a roll of 35mm film.

TIP: MEMORY CARDS & WRITE SPEED

When deciding which brand of memory card is best, consider the *write speed*. The faster/higher the write speed, the less time your camera's image processor will spend processing an exposure (writing the data) and the faster it will send it to the LCD screen for viewing.

Most memory cards use the same formula for data transfer rates as the CD-Rom industry—a data transfer rate of 1X equals 150 kilobytes (KB) per second. So, a memory card that offers an 80X write speed is faster than one that offers a 40X write speed—and, of course, you pay a bit more for speed. *And note*: All things being equal, your camera's processor speed is of equal importance; your processor must be able to write at the speed listed on the memory card; if it can't write at as fast a speed as listed on a card, it doesn't make sense to buy that faster card.

ISO

What exactly do I mean by ISO? In pure technical speak, ISO stands for International Organization for Standardization, more commonly referred to as International Standards Organization (good to know since someday you may be on *Jeopardy*). In film photography, the ISO rating indicates a film's sensitivity to light. In digital photography, it indicates the digital sensor's sensitivity to light. But most importantly, the ISO lets your digital camera's light meter know exactly what combinations of aperture and shutter speed it can use to record an exposure.

In the early days of photography, there was never a built-in light meter, and as a result, there was never a setting on the camera for ISO. A handheld light meter was required for all picture-taking efforts, and it was on this handheld light meter that one would set the ISO, selecting the ISO number that corresponded with the ISO of the film in the camera. It wasn't until the late 1960s—when light meters were first installed *inside* camera bodies—that ISO became part of the camera controls.

By default, most digital cameras today come right out of the box with the ISO set to the lowest number—100, 125, or 200 depending on the camera. So, does this mean that you never have to worry about setting the ISO? Not necessarily. Let me explain. Without light—and I mean *no* light whatsoever—your digital camera would never make an exposure. That goes for all cameras—not just digital cameras. It has been true since the invention of photography. Every photographic image that was ever made and will ever be made needs light. Only the format of the medium changes. Up until now, the medium used for capturing light has been film; but for many of us today, that medium is now a digital sensor.

As I said earlier, the pixels are the "image makers" that record an image, but pixels cannot even begin to record an image unless you indicate the ISO with which they should be working. When you select an ISO, your camera records every picture at that ISO until you tell it otherwise. Once you change that setting from, say, ISO 400 to ISO 125, your camera will record every subsequent image at that ISO until you it otherwise.

Why would you want to change the ISO? Because the ISO has a direct effect on the speed at which the pixels gather up data and record an image. As far as pixels are concerned, the ISO is like caffeine. Imagine that ISO 125 represents 125mg of caffeine. And, let's say that this is the "normal" dose of caffeine under which the pixels operate. Now imagine how much quicker the pixels could record an image if they were given a stronger dose of caffeine such as 400mg—in other words, ISO 400. The higher the ISO number, the faster the ISO and

the more sensitive it is to light. A faster, more light-sensitive ISO is better at capturing a fast-moving or a dimly lit subject.

Of course, you don't always want a fast ISO. Feeding pixels too much caffeine does have its drawbacks. It can rob them of "sleep," and before you know it their "eyes" are "bloodshot." Those bloodshot eyes show up in your pictures as *noise*, a grainy texture. The higher the ISO, the noisier the picture will be. This is the same grain you may have experienced if you shot high-speed film, such as ISO 400 or 800.

Does this mean that you should use a faster ISO because you're in a hurry? Of course not. But again, if your subject is in a hurry—like that fast-moving kayaker shooting down the rapids—and you want to freeze the action in sharply focused detail, then using the fast ISO may be a good idea.

Due to high ISOs' light sensitivity, you can also—although I'm not one who espouses fast ISOs for this purpose—use them when photographing cityscapes in low light at dusk without a tripod, but I'll explain my opposition to this approach in the section on shutter speed (see pages 52–63). But since tripod use is not allowed in many interior locations—like cathedrals and art museums—I would recommend shooting at high ISOs, such as 400 or 640.

Digital technology affords digital photographers some liberties of which film photographers could only dream, the biggest one being the ease with which you can switch from one ISO setting to another. Once you've taken that close-up of the flower in the park at ISO 125, you simply switch to ISO 400 to freeze the action of your daughter jumping rope nearby. In effect, it's like changing from one roll of film to another but without the hassle of rewinding and reloading film cassettes. How easy is it to switch the ISO? You simply push a button and/or rotate a dial on your camera—it takes all of two seconds.

Using a high ISO for any sports-related subject is often a good idea, *if you want to render the image in crisp, sharp detail.* To get this shot, I crouched down low and, with ISO 640, handheld my camera as the skateboarder came flying out of the "bowl" behind him and up and over this garbage can. With my shutter speed set to a 1/500 second, I adjusted my aperture until f/13 indicated a correct exposure.

12–24mm lens, 1/500 sec. at f/13

ISO FLEXIBILTY VS. NOISE

Imagine you're on vacation in Europe and you just shot a number of images of the flowering cherry trees outside the famous Nôtre Dame Cathedral in Paris. You've been using ISO 125 all morning and your wife suggests that you now go inside the cathedral for a look. Once inside, you realize it's far too dark to take a handheld shot of the interior, but by simply switching your ISO from 125 to 640, you discover that you can now take the exposure at a shutter speed that's safe to handhold. And yes, there's that downside to a high ISO: noise. But most of us can live with the noise, especially if our only other choice is not to take the shot altogether.

Noise is *not* the issue it once was either, as there are now more than four or five software programs on the market that reduce noise when processing your images in the computer. In addition, camera manufacturers have also made recent strides in reducing noise at the moment the image is recorded via a *noise reduction feature* found on many of the new DSLRs.

The ease of shifting from one ISO to another also has a potential downside, which is that you may forget to return to a lower, more commonly used ISO setting (say 100, 125, or 200) after you're done shooting the ISO 640 low-light shots. Perhaps you get caught in a conversation inside the cathedral, and once you return outside, you continue your walk until another photo opportunity catches your attention. It may not be until day's end that you realize that the additional forty-seven pictures you took after leaving the church were also shot on ISO 640. This is one time when digital *cannot* save you. Once you record any image at a particular ISO, that image is forever "stuck" with that ISO—even if you're shooting in raw format.

ISO has a direct effect on the speed at which the pixels gather up data and record an image. As far as pixels are concerned, it's like caffeine.

There are many interior locations where tripods are either not practical or, perhaps, not even allowed. I was able to take this shot inside a cathedral handheld, thanks to the ease of changing my ISO, which I set to 800. The downside of using a high ISO, however, can be noise (that fine graininess that permeates this entire composition). At the present time, just as with graininess in film, noise appears to be here to stay—but I wouldn't bet the farm on it. With the rapid pace of digital technology, we will one day soon see less and less noise with even the highest ISO numbers.

Noise and its related anomalies are also a common occurrence when using exposure times that are longer than 8 seconds. There was a time when there was no quick fix for these problems, but with noise reduction software programs (like Kodak Digital Gem Noise Reduction, a plug-in I added to my Photoshop software), these effects can be quickly vanquished.

12–24mm lens, f/4 for 1/60 sec.

WHITE BALANCE

Are you confused about white balance? It's my opinion that, next to the histogram, the white balance setting is one of the most overrated controls on the digital camera. I have actually seen forums on the Internet discussing white balance, and there are some very strong feelings about the importance of white balance in your image-making. But, until someone can really show me otherwise, I will continue setting my white balance only *once* and leaving it alone.

Before I get to what, exactly, white balance is and to my one chosen setting, I want to briefly discuss the colors red, green, and blue, and color temperature. Every color picture ever made has some degree of each of these colors in it, but how much will depend on the color temperature of the light. Yes, that's right. Light, just like the human body, has a temperature. Unlike the human body, though, the temperature of light is measured by its color. And this is where it gets kind of funny. Blue light has a higher temperature than red light in photography. If you were red in the face, you'd probably also have sweat coming out of your pores, and anyone who looked at you would say, "You're burning up!"

Not so, with the temperature of light. Color temperature is measured by what is called the Kelvin scale, which is nothing more than an extension of the Celsius scale. On any given day, the color temperature of the light that falls on our world is measured in degrees Kelvin (K), from roughly 2,000 K to 11,000 K. A color temperature of between 7,000 and 11,000 K is considered "cool" (bluer shades would fall in this range), a color temperature of between 2,000 and 4,000 K is considered "warm" (reds would fall in this range), and a color temperature of between 4,000 and 7,000 K is considered "daylight" (or the combination of red, green, and blue).

Cool light is found on cloudy, rainy, foggy, or snowy days, or in areas of open shade on sunny days (the north side of your house, for example). Warm light is found on sunny days, beginning a bit before dawn and lasting for about two hours tops, and then beginning again about two hours before sunset and lasting for another twenty or thirty minutes after the sun has set. The light generated by the 60-watt lamp bulbs inside your house on a winter's morning or a summer's eve is also warm light. (That's why, when you used daylight film indoors without flash everyone looked like they paid a visit to a bad tanning salon.)

Today's digital cameras would have you believe that, with every lighting situation, you should turn your white balance control to that specific color temperature before you shoot. But how are you to know the exact color temperature unless you have a color temperature meter? And, a good one will cost you about eight hundred dollars, as of this writing. Well, fortunately, you don't need a meter, since the simplest way to get the "right" white balance is to put an 8 x 10-inch bright white card out in the front of the lens every time you move from one lighting condition to the next. This way, your camera will know exactly where it needs to set the white balance, and, by golly, this way you're assured of getting "perfect" color.

This is the train of thought shared by many, but it's one train I won't be riding, and here's why: I love color! As a once-die-hard film shooter, I shot 90 percent of all my images with the most saturated films available at any given time. During my last six years of using film, I made 90 percent of my images with Kodak's E100VS, a highly saturated color slide film. One of the problems I had with digital photography in the beginning was its inability to produce in the raw file these same highly saturated colors—until I stumbled upon the Cloudy white balance setting, that is.

Over the years, I found myself out shooting film in overcast, rainy, snowy, foggy, or open-shade/sunny-day conditions. To eliminate much of the blue light present at those times, I would use my 81-A or 81-B warming filters. These would add red to a scene, in effect knocking down, if not out, the blue light. I prefer my images warm.

And that brings me to my one white balance (WB) setting. As was the case with my Nikon D1X digital camera, and now with my Nikon D2X, I leave the white balance set to Cloudy +3. If you own a Nikon D-70 and D-100, you can also set the WB to Cloudy and add +3 via the fine-tuning button.

On Canon cameras, you're given a choice of color temperatures, and when setting the WB to Cloudy, you can fine-tune it by also setting the color temperature to 6300 K. If your camera doesn't offer any additional fine-tuning beyond the Cloudy setting, no worries. But at the least, set it to Cloudy and leave it there. If—and this is a *big if*—you feel that the Cloudy WB setting is a bit too much, you can always change it to Auto or Daylight or Shade or Tungsten or Fluorescent or Flash in the post-processing phase, assuming, of course, that you're shooting in raw mode. (This is yet another good reason to shoot raw files.)

Perhaps you are shocked by my WB choice, but hear me out. I seldom, if ever, shoot interiors, whether they are lit by available daylight, tungsten, fluorescent, sodium, or mercury vapor. I'm a natural light photographer, as are probably most of you reading this book. The only exceptions to this are when I use my mini-studio setup at home to photograph objects on white backgrounds, and when I'm doing commercial work for which I'm using a number of strobes to light a given interior. In both of these situations, I usually end up using the Flash setting for white balance. I'm also a very specific-time-of-day photographer. On sunny days, I shoot in the early morning or from late afternoon to dusk. Midday light, between 11:00 a.m. and 3:00 p.m., is what I call *poolside light*, and if there's a pool nearby, that's where you'll find me: sitting by the pool, with sun block, of course.

So, since I add even more warmth with my white balance set to Cloudy +3, it's like shooting with Kodak E100VS. And my white balance never changes, whether I shoot on sunny, cloudy, rainy, foggy, or snowy days. And, in case you're convinced that I'm truly an idiot, don't forget that if I determine, on those rarest of occasions—and I want to stress *rare*—that I may have been better off with a different WB setting, I can always change *any* white balance setting in post-processing after downloading my raw images into the computer.

If more photographers would follow my advice, especially those who are not morning or late-afternoon-to-dusk shooters, they would be amazed at the warmth in the pictures that they take while I'm poolside. Midday photography is the norm for many, and the added warmth that you'll see in your pictures (that's normally associated with early or late times of day) will surely get your attention. You can fool your friends into thinking you've become a morning person, or that you were out shooting in late afternoon light, but be careful for the discerning eye. Morning and late afternoon light reveal lots of long shadows, while midday light is "shadowless." And if you're thinking of taking on the intricate task of adding shadows later in Photoshop, you might consider volunteering for the Peace Corps instead if you have that much time on your hands.

The image on the left is a classic example of midday light, made with the camera set to the Auto white balance setting, which not surprisingly did a "great" job of recording accurate color; and since midday light is blue, it looks blue overall. Now compare this to the other image (right), which I made with the white balance set to Cloudy +3. Obviously, this image is warmer. The choice is, of course, a personal one, but if you have not considered shooting with your white balance set to Cloudy, it might be worth a look.

Both photos: 17–55mm lens at 24mm, f/16 for 1/125 sec.

INFRARED "FILM"

Just when you thought digital couldn't get any better, it does! There's a good chance your digital camera can also shoot infrared "film" (i.e., in Infrared mode), too. If you're not sure, then put it to this simple test: Place your camera on one end of the kitchen table, set the metering mode to Aperture Priority, and the aperture to $f/22$. Go get the TV remote, and, assuming that like most remotes, it works on an infrared beam, place it at the other end of the table. Now, go back to your camera and with the lens set to around 50–70mm, focus on the remote. Set the camera's self-timer, run down to the other end of the table, push the button on the remote and keep it pushed while your camera takes an exposure. Look at your LCD screen. If it shows either a faint or a vivid dot from the remote, then your camera will shoot infrared images.

As far as shooting infrared images, it is *not* the same world as color or black-and-white photography. Since infrared light is invisible to the human eye (without special eyewear), you will quickly discover two necessities when shooting infrared images: (1) an infrared filter, and (2) a real understanding of which subjects are best-suited to the infrared mode.

Due to the differences between how each brand of digital camera sees infrared, I can't recommend which one infrared filter will work best for you. Talk with the people at your local professional camera store, or jump on the Internet and do a simple Web search; a search under "infrared photography" will certainly yield a wealth of information. Having said that, it's a safe bet that most, if not all, of you could head out the door tomorrow and get satisfactory, if not great, photographic results with the use of the Hoya R72 filter. According to my many students, this one filter has opened the door to some amazing discoveries in infrared image-making.

So, out the door you go with your digital infrared camera, but hold on a minute. Infrared light waves are invisible to the human eye, so if you can't see them, how do you know where to focus? Once again, more good news: With the filter in place, the camera can now "see" infrared light waves, and the autofocus mechanism of your camera/lens does a great job of this for you.

And what about setting the exposure? First of all, I prefer to work with ISO 100 to ISO 200, even when shooting infrared images. As you'll discover, the infrared filter is almost black, so light levels are drastically reduced and, as such, exposure times may be long—depending, of course, on your aperture. But more importantly, get accustomed to using your tripod, because most infrared work (unless you're working at midday and with wide open apertures) will require exposure times of 1/15 sec. and slower—again depending on aperture and time of day. It's all about experimentation and a lot of trial and error. That's why you should bracket every shot, at least on the plus side, one or two stops, until you get used to the many nuances of shooting with infrared.

WHAT'S BRACKETING?

Some examples of bracketing would be: You're shooting in manual exposure mode, and after you define what your exposure will be, say $f/8$ for 1/15 sec., you take another image for 1/8 sec. and another for 1/4 sec.—both the while leaving the camera at $f/8$. Or, you can shoot in autoexposure mode, but after the first shot, adjust your autoexposure override to +1 and take another shot and then adjust it to +2 and take one more. Here again, your camera's LCD screen can come into play by giving you an idea of which exposure looks best.

Also, a common question I get in my courses is whether or not to leave the camera set for color or black and white when shooting infrared images. It's my suggestion that you leave it at color—you can always do the conversion to black and white when you download the raw file to the computer. And although the camera's LCD screen cannot show you a truly clear picture of your images, it is easier to see the results of your exposure in color than in black and white.

And finally, does any subject make a good infrared image? Again, trial and error is the rule, but since infrared light waves are the strongest with green subjects, don't be surprised if you migrate toward trees, grass, and springtime wheat fields.

Infrared is not the same world as color or black-and-white photography.

WHAT'S THE BLOCKING FILTER?

Unlike traditional daylight-appropriate films, your image sensor is quite sensitive to infrared light waves. And that's why most, if not all, sensors leave the factory with a blocking filter designed to block infrared light. However, most blocking filters will still allow enough infrared light to pass through and onto the sensor so that you can, in fact, record infrared images.

An unassuming street scene

in France takes on a surreal quality when photographed with an infrared filter. The normal daylight color exposure was, quite honestly, nothing to write home about (top). But, when I shot this same color image using the infrared filter, an electric red color resulted (center). The exposure time was *f*/16 for 1 second. This is a *color* infrared image, and although it's definitely different than daylight color, it's still not the truly surreal look for which infrared is noted. Only after converting the image to black and white in Photoshop do you see the truly compelling infrared version (bottom). It's an entirely different and more positive response. As my wife was quick to remark once I had processed the image, "Wow, it looks like snow!"

Top: 18–55mm lens, f/16 for 1/60 sec.
Center: 18–55mm lens, f/16 for 1 second

APERTURE

APERTURE'S TRUE IMPORTANCE

As you'll notice, throughout this book I've listed which lens, aperture (*f*-stop), and shutter speed I used for every photograph. Perhaps you're wondering why I used *f*/4 or *f*/6.3 for some, *f*/8 or *f*/11 for others, and *f*/16 or *f*/36 for still others. Why the different apertures? Why not just use one and stay with it? Because, quite simply, I want to *create* exposures, not *make* exposures. Your aperture choice can have a profound effect on an image's overall outcome.

Aperture has two functions, and the first is the more familiar to most shooters: to control the volume of light that passes through the lens and onto the awaiting Pixel family. The pixels then take this light and record an image. But there's a bit more to an aperture than simply being a hole in your lens that allows light to pass through—and is it ever important!

The second—the real and true—importance of aperture is its ability affect the sharpness of an image. It can render an amazing amount of sharpness that spans from just a few feet away all the way to infinity, or it can render only a select area of sharpness that begins and ends on whatever you have chosen to focus. In photographic terms this area of sharpness from front to back in an image is called *depth of field*.

No matter what you choose to shoot, at some point you have to focus on something, or if you're using autofocus, the camera will focus on something for you. Once something has been focused on, and depending on the composition, you may notice that there are areas beyond and/or in front of this chosen focal point that *are not sharp*. This is where it gets interesting. Do you want everything in your picture to be sharp, from front to back? Or, do you want to only render the focal point in sharp focus?

The real and true importance of aperture is its ability to affect the sharpness of an image.

These are two identical exposures, but they have two unique messages. And it's the aperture—and *only* the aperture—that is controlling the *visual weight* here. The compositions are identical. As a rule, whatever is in focus is perceived by the eye/brain as of greater importance than whatever is not in focus, and again, it is the aperture that controls, for the most part, this visual weight.

Which do you prefer? What's important here is that it's not so much that one is right and one is wrong, but rather that you understand that when you choose the right aperture for the composition, your pictures will have *impact*! By choosing the right aperture, you make it clear to the viewer what message you want to convey.

Top: 17–55mm lens at 40mm, f/4 for 1/640 sec.
Bottom: 17–55mm lens at 40mm, f/22 for 1/20 sec.

F/22, STORYTELLING, AND THE WIDE-ANGLE LENS

Assuming you want everything, from front to back, in in your composition to be sharp, the laws of depth of field would require you to use the smallest aperture openings, such as f/16 or f/22. (If you think about how you squint to try to make something appear sharper to your eye, you get an idea of why you need a smaller aperture opening to render this greater depth of field.) And what kind of subject come to mind for which you might want everything sharp? The most common response is, of course, nature—specifically, landscapes.

We've all done our share of ooohing and ahhhhhhing at those amazing images—of, say, a field of wildflowers in the foreground leading to a lake and then to some vast and distant mountains in the background—where everything is tack sharp, front to back. For a subject like this, exacting sharpness is king! How on earth did the photographer do that? It must have been one of those really expensive cameras, no doubt. Truth be told, you and almost everyone else reading this book already has one of those "really expensive cameras." Read on.

These kinds of pictures are what I call *storytelling* imagery, and just like the name implies, these images do a really great job of telling a story. Like any good story, there is a beginning (the foreground subject, such as the flowers just mentioned), a middle (the lake), and an ending (the vast mountain range). In effect, an aperture of f/22 tells this kind of story, allowing for the beginning, middle, and end to all be expressed thoroughly and in complete detail.

In order to allow for as much visual information as possible, you want to use a lens that captures the widest possible view. Not surprisingly, the most favored lens choice of serious amateurs and pros alike for making these compelling storytelling images is the wide-angle lens. Simply put, if you're using the increasingly popular 12–24mm lens or the "standard" 18–55mm or 18–70mm lenses (or if you're using a wide-angle lens from your film days, such as a 17–35mm or 20–35mm), you definitely have the right lens to tell some amazing stories. But it will also help you to know exactly which of these focal lengths work best to create these wonderful storytelling images.

With a 12–24mm zoom lens, you'll call upon the 12–16mm range. With an 18–55mm, an 18–70mm, a 17–35mm, or a 20–35mm, you'll only call on the 17–18mm range. It is within these focal lengths that the angle of view allows you to create those wide and sweeping storytelling compositions.

There are several reasons why these wide-angle focal lengths are the most favored, and they do offer the greatest angle of view, allowing the photographer to compose more subject matter in the scene. But—and this is crucial—it is absolutely imperative that you *choose the right aperture* to go along with these wide angles of view. If you do that, you'll be assured of recording pictures that, up until now, you thought were only possible with a more expensive camera or for which you thought you needed much more know-how.

In other words, these incredible landscape compositions have to do, in part, with the angle of the lens (the wider the better), laying down low, or getting up very close to the foreground (your point of view), but the real secret is this: You will never render the whole story in exacting sharpness and detail, from the immediate foreground to the distant horizon, unless you use the right aperture! And, again, what is the right aperture for *all* storytelling landscapes? There is but one, and it is f/22—and every wide-angle lens or wide-angle zoom lens made for a DSLR or an SLR has an aperture of f/22.

A NOTE ABOUT APERTURE NUMBERS

It can be confusing at first, but keep in mind that small aperture openings are indicated by larger f-stop numbers, while large aperture openings are indicated by smaller f-stop numbers. So, an aperture of f/22, for example, is smaller than an aperture of f/16.

Along the banks of the many canals in West Freisland, Holland, you'll find the occasional windmill. Although there once were over twenty thousand windmills along these dikes, there are but several hundred remaining today. Since this was a sidelit scene, I used my polarizing filter to render the sky a deeper blue and also to remove the harsh glare from the somewhat shiny trees and grasses. It's only with sidelit subjects that the maximum benefit of a polarizing filter is realized. I then chose f/22, pointed the camera toward the blue sky, and adjusted my shutter speed until 1/20 sec. indicated a correct exposure. I used a tripod, chose the focal length of 16mm, and preset the focus to 3 feet. Finding a frame within the picture frame, I purposely sought out this foreground of tall grasses and trees with which to frame the background windmill, thereby elevating its importance. Although the background didn't appear sharp in the viewfinder, the use of f/22 rendered the front-to-back depth of field needed. You might notice the absence of sharpness in the upper tree branches, but this is simply the result of a slight breeze that moved the branches.

12–24mm lens at 16mm, f/22 for 1/20 sec.

STORYTELLING AND THE WIDE-ANGLE LENS

Chances are good that you'd feel shortchanged if you bought a book in which the first nine pages were blank. Yet, this is how many photographers "write" their storytelling images: with the photographic equivalent of blank pages—*empty foregrounds*. And, for obvious reasons, these images are seldom compelling. To avoid recording empty foregrounds, you *must* move in close to that foreground.

Most photographers aren't inclined to think of the wide-angle lens as a close-up lens, but if they did, their images would improve tenfold. When shooting wide and sweeping scenes, the tendency is to step back so that you can get more stuff in the picture's composition. Big mistake! From now on, try to get in the habit of stepping closer—closer to the foreground flowers, closer to the foreground trees, closer to the foreground rocks. Embrace the "one-foot rule": If you are one foot from the flowers, tree trunk, sandy shoreline, or rocky outcroppings, you are assured of filling up the first nine pages of your story with "text."

FOOLPROOF FOCUSING FORMULA

My students often wonder where to focus when making storytelling compositions. Try my foolproof "formula." It's guaranteed to work each and every time. First, you must turn off the autofocus. If your lens has a 75-degree angle of view (18mm on the digital 18–55mm zoom), first set the aperture to *f*/22, and then focus on something that's approximately 5 feet from the lens. Then, if you're in manual exposure mode, adjust your shutter speed until a correct exposure is indicated and shoot; if you're in Aperture Priority mode, simply shoot, since the camera will set the shutter speed for you.

If you're using a 12–24mm digital wide-angle zoom lens, and your focal length is between 12mm and 16mm, set the lens to *f*/22 and focus on something 3 feet away and repeat the final steps mentioned above.

If you're using a digital point-and-shoot camera, you can use an aperture of *f*/8 or even *f*/5.6, and if you can't turn the autofocus off, then autofocus on something 5 feet from the lens. Use the autofocus lock, and then recompose the scene you want to shoot.

Now chances are, you might be skeptical the first time you use this technique, since you'll certainly notice that the landscape, overall, doesn't look the least bit sharp throughout when you look through your viewfinder. Trust me on this, though—it will be sharp, from front to back. And because you have the LCD screen on the back of your camera, you can check this there for yourself. The only reason it doesn't appear in sharp focus in the viewfinder is because you're used to viewing wide-open apertures through the lens (i.e., *f*/2.8, *f*/3.5, or *f*/4 depending on the lens) and not the much smaller storytelling aperture of *f*/22.

TIP: LET THE CAMERA DO THE WORK (IF IT CAN)

You may have a camera that will calculate the depth of field for you—Canon has several cameras that do this. Check your camera manual to learn how to turn on and use this feature. Basically what happens is this: You let the camera focus on that portion of the foreground that you want sharp, and then you let it focus on the distant horizon. The camera will then remember these two distances, and assuming it is within the depth-of-field range for *f*/22 at your given focal length, it will "let you" take the picture. If you have trouble figuring out how to do this, you can always use the Foolproof Focusing Formula above.

I was in Cancun photographing staff for a corporate client. When I finally got a free afternoon, I quickly rushed out to buy a large conch shell from a local vendor near the beach and placed it in the foregrounds of the many beach shots I made that day. Staging photographs isn't uncommon for me, *if* I can make it believable. Not so much believable to other photographers but to the general public, since the market for an image like this would be folks who like to travel.

To get this image, I knelt at the ocean's edge, placed the shell before me, and set the focal length to 15mm and the aperture to *f*/22. With my camera set to Aperture Priority mode, I simply aimed, focused on the shell, and shot, allowing the camera to choose 1/90 sec. as the correct exposure.

12–24mm lens at 15mm, f/22 for 1/90 sec.

With my camera and 12–24mm lens on a tripod, I set the aperture to *f*/22 and focused on these foreground flowers, which were about three feet away. The image above shows how the overall image looked through the viewfinder, and as you can see, it was anything but sharp. However, I didn't worry, since only when you press the shutter release does the lens actually stop down to the selected aperture of *f*/22. And as the second example on the opposite page shows, the desired storytelling sharpness from front to back is evident. Unlike the film shooter, who must now wait for the film to be processed to be really sure if "this work," the digital photographer can immediately tell the desired sharpness was attained by simply looking in the monitor.

Opposite: 12–24mm lens, f/22 for 1/15 sec.

You will never render the whole story in exacting sharpness and detail, from the immediate foreground to the distant horizon, unless you use the right aperture!

THE DIGITAL CONVERSION FACTOR

I f you're using some, or all, of the same lenses from your film camera on your new digital SLR, you have, no doubt, become familiar with the increased focal lengths in those lenses when placed on the digital SLR. This is due to the *conversion factor* of now having those lenses attached to a camera with a smaller "film" size than 35mm (i.e., the image sensor).

It's easy to embrace this optical trait when you are using your 70–300mm lens, since it converts to a 100–420mm zoom. But it is, perhaps, a hard pill to swallow when your 20–35mm wide-angle zoom lens becomes, roughly, a 28–50mm zoom. The response by the industry to this rude awakening has been the very popular 12–24mm wide-angle zoom lens. And the consumer has been so quick to respond

to this lens that it is still very hard to find it in stock at many camera stores.

On a brighter note, despite the transformation to an increased focal length and subsequent decrease in the angle of view in these lenses, *the depth of field properties of these lenses have not changed one iota*. Your 20–35mm zoom can still render depth of field from, roughly, 18 inches to infinity when set to 20mm and shot at f/22, even though the angle of view has decreased from 92 degrees to 75 degrees. And what is true of any wide-angle lens originally meant for a 35mm film camera is also true of any telephoto lens originally meant for a 35mm film camera: The focal length of your "digital" 70–300mm lens has changed, but it still has the depth of field of a "film camera" 70–300mm lens.

STORYTELLING AND POINT-AND-SHOOT CAMERAS

If you're using a digital point-and-shoot camera, almost all of your apertures are storytelling apertures. The digital point-and-shoot is hopelessly endowed with a tremendous amount of depth of field, even at those aperture numbers that are normally associated with a short depth of field, such as $f/4$ or $f/5.6$. The downside of this is that it's difficult at best to isolate a subject without resorting to using a close-up attachment.

The upside of this is that you can record storytelling compositions at larger aperture openings, such as $f/5.6$ or $f/8$, rendering the same large depth of field normally associated with $f/16$ or $f/22$ on a digital SLR. Where the digital SLR shooter may have to resort to using a tripod, due to the smaller lens openings, photographers with digital point-and-shoot cameras are more than likely able to handhold their camera to capture many of their storytelling compositions—since exposure times are faster when using larger lens openings.

Having said this, it's also important to note that, as you may have already learned about your digital point-and-shoot camera, it comes up short in the wide-angle/storytelling lens arena. Most storytelling compositions rely on a wide-angle lens with a minimum angle of view of 75 degrees, and as of this writing, more than 90 percent of the digital point-and-shoot cameras offer up an angle of view no wider than 62 degrees. It's not that you can't record compositions with vast depth of fields, but you will do so within a limited angle of view. And yes, I'm aware that some of these point-and-shoots, such as the Nikon 8700, offer up an auxiliary lens to make the angle of view wider, but by the time you spend the money on the attachment and the camera itself, you could have bought Nikon's popular digital SLR—the Nikon D-70—with an 18–70mm lens for about the same price or Canon's digital Rebel with an 18–55mm lens for even less!

STORYTELLING AND TELEPHOTO LENSES

Although the telephoto lens is seldom used for storytelling compositions, it can be. But when using the telephoto lens for this type of image, photographers are often perplexed as to where to focus. The general rule is this: Once you've framed the subject and set the aperture to the largest f-stop number (the smallest opening)—$f/22$ or $f/32$—simply focus one-third of the way into the scene and then shoot.

*T*he digital point-and-shoot camera is hopelessly endowed with a tremendous amount of depth of field. . . .The upside of this is that you can record storytelling compositions at larger aperture openings.

Focusing one-third of the way into the scene is exactly what I did one evening while photographing this pedestrian bridge in France shortly after sunset. I used a tripod for stability during the long exposure and focused on the second archway on the bridge. The overall magenta color cast in the image came courtesy of the FLW filter I often use when shooting cityscapes or landscapes at dawn and dusk.

80–200mm lens at 110mm, f/22 for 2 seconds

ISOLATION APERTURES

f we think of *f/22* and the wide-angle lens as the story-telling aperture and lens, then *f/4* or *f/5.6* and the telephoto lens can be thought of as the *isolating apertures* and lens. Keeping with the storytelling and writing analogy, an isolating aperture is like a highlighter pen that flags a key word or phrase in a particular story. I refer to pictures that highlight just one subject as *isolation* or *singular-theme* imagery. It is the telephoto lens and the smaller aperture numbers (*f/4* or *f/5.6*, which are actually larger aperture *openings*, remember) that are the best combinations to use

Every New Yorker has a "taxicab" story to tell. The New York City taxi is synonymous with both humor and frustration, so much so that it earned its own sit-com, *Taxi*, which, as everyone knows, was a smash hit.

In terms of sheer numbers, the area around Times Square in New York City looks like a taxi convention! I was drawn to this particular taxi simply because of the illuminated off-duty sign—a sign anyone needing a cab hates to see. With my camera mounted on a tripod and a focal length of 350mm, I was able to zero in on just the off-duty light but still communicate a sense of place by including the Roxy Deli sign in the background. Yet, by using a large lens opening (*f/5.6*), I was able to limit the sign's visual weight and ensure that it remained a secondary element. This is a perfect example of how attention to detail can't be overstated; if I had used an aperture of *f/22*, both the off-duty sign and the Roxy sign would have been clear—and would have been fighting for attention. You should use the telephoto lens to place emphasis on whatever you've chosen to be the main point of interest in the composition.

Right: 80–400mm lens at 350mm, f/5.6

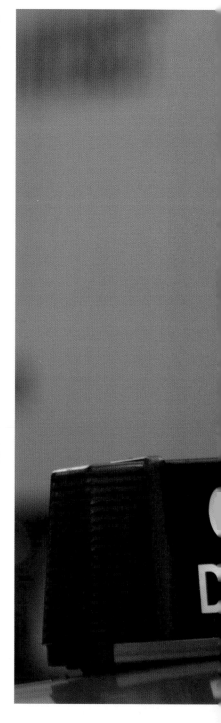

for isolating a subject since they limit the depth of field within a scene. When you combine a singular-theme aperture with a singular-theme lens, you're all but guaranteed success with your isolation images!

Unlike the wide-angle lens, which has an "open mind" and can see everything—in other words, it has a great angle of view—the telephoto lens is "very narrow-minded" due to its limited angle of view. When you combine, say, an 80–400mm telephoto lens (with an angle of view ranging from 25 degrees to a meager 6 degrees) with an aperture that yields narrow, isolating, or shallow depth of field (like *f*/4 or *f*/5.6), you can focus on just the one or two details you want to extract from an otherwise chaotic world. In effect, the isolation apertures and the telephoto lens are capable of pointing out the finer points and details that are often hidden in many storytelling compositions.

While visiting a nursery, I came upon several large potted hibiscus plants. Reaching immediately for my camera and tripod, I began framing up a flower approximately seven feet away (boxed detail left). To isolate the flower for the final image, I made sure to also include several petals from a few flowers that were a mere six inches from the lens. I then chose an aperture of *f*/4, thus limiting the depth of field to the one main flower and throwing the foreground petals out of focus (above).

80–400mm lens, f/4 for 1/320 sec.

ISOLATION APERTURES & THE WIDE-ANGLE LENS

The wide-angle lens is seldom thought of as a lens that's capable of isolating a subject. Due to its natural ability to encompass a large angle of view, thereby getting a lot of stuff in the frame, it just doesn't make sense for isolating—at least, that's what many photographers believe. A wide-angle lens does have the uncanny ability to focus close, however, and when you combine this close-up vision with isolation or singular-theme apertures, some quite striking—as well as informative—photographic compositions can result.

This photograph has certainly an isolated or singular theme: a kiss. Yet, it also displays some background subject matter that gives it an added boost. I handheld the camera for this wide-angle close-up and was using my 17–55mm lens with the focal length at 26mm (an effective 62-degree angle of view).

17–55mm lens at 26mm, f/5.6 for 1/125 sec.

Although seldom thought of as being capable of isolating a subject, the wide-angle lens does have the uncanny ability to focus close.

"WHO CARES?" APERTURES

Okay, simple enough: You can shoot storytelling imagery with small aperture openings and singular-theme imagery with big aperture openings. But is there ever a time when you don't have to worry about choosing the right aperture?

If you're familiar with my last book, you know that the answer to that is yes. In fact, there are many wonderful exposures/compositions to be made with nary a care in the world about aperture choice, and I refer to these picture-taking opportunities as *"Who cares?"* aperture choices. *Who cares* what aperture you use when photographing a subject against a brick wall, since the subject and the wall are at the *same* focal distance? *Who cares* what aperture you use when shooting straight down on a composition of fallen autumn leaves, since the leaves and the ground are at the same focal distance? Who cares what aperture you use when capturing

Although the purpose of any traffic light is to control traffic flow, it can also be a place of refuge for pigeons. With my 80–400mm lens and camera on a tripod, I was able to isolate just the traffic light and pigeons from an otherwise busy and chaotic cityscape. An added bonus was having the traffic light in open shade yet set against the much brighter background of blue sky. With my aperture set to *f*/11 (Who cares?), I adjusted my shutter speed until 1/200 sec. indicated a correct exposure from the brighter blue sky. This exposure choice rendered the stark shapes you see opposite as silhouettes, yet it also proved to be a correct exposure for the red light. (With this one exposure, I was able to show both a "Who cares?" aperture and a single-theme image.)

a distant hot-air balloon floating against the clear blue sky, since the balloon and sky are at the same focal distance?

Although you can make these kinds of exposures/compositions easily at any aperture, and despite my affection for calling them "Who cares?" images, I would like to recommend that you use apertures of $f/8$ or $f/11$. If you're using a digital point-and-shoot camera, use $f/4$ or $f/5.6$. Why? Because these apertures let you take advantage of your lens's "sweet spot." Every lens offers the greatest edge-to-edge sharpness and contrast at apertures of $f/8$ to $f/11$ (or $f/4$ to $f/5.6$ with digital point-and-shoot cameras), hence the term *sweet spot*.

This sweet spot seldom offers up enough depth of field for effective storytelling compositions and often produces far too much depth of field for singular-theme compositions. But as I've said, the world isn't made up entirely of storytelling and singular-theme subjects. There are just as many—if not more—"Who cares?" exposures waiting to be taken too, and when coming upon "Who cares?" compositions, I will always choose apertures from $f/8$ to $f/11$.

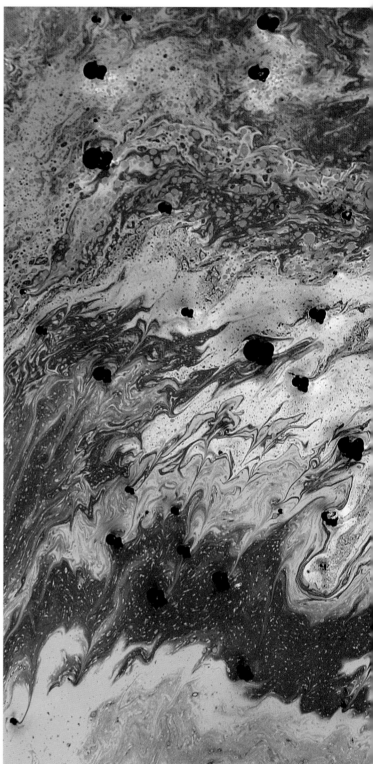

If you want to try your hand at "easy" exposures, grab your camera and an 18–55mm zoom lens and head out the door, with your tripod of course—and pay close attention to what lies on the street as you walk. Chances are, whatever you find at your feet can be shot effectively at *f*/8 or *f*/11. And who knows, maybe you'll make some unexpected discoveries, as I have over the years. It's amazing what most people don't even notice at their feet!

How long it had been there was anybody's guess, but this crushed Schweppes can lying on the ground was reason enough to frame a "Who cares?" exposure. With my camera and 35–70mm lens on a tripod, and my aperture set to *f*/11, I was able to simply frame, focus, and shoot since I was also in Aperture Priority mode.

35–70mm lens, f/11 for 1/30 sec.

Not far away from the Schweppes can, I came upon a parked moving van whose engine had been leaking oil. With the recent rain shower, the leaking oil had been transformed into a "landscape" that looked like something that might have been taken by the Mars space probe. Again, with the camera and lens on a tripod, and the aperture set to *f*/11, I was able to simply frame, focus, and shoot since I was also in Aperture Priority mode.

35–70mm lens, f/11 for 1/8 sec.

SUMMARY: LENS COMPARISION

What is the most obvious differences in these three images? The overall angle of view is certainly one difference and so is the subsequent depth of field. All three images were shot at the same aperture and shutter speed: $f/8$ for 1/350 sec. All three images share a similar composition in that the baby fills up approximately the same space in the frame. But, note the *vast* difference in the angles of view. I took the first image with my 12–24mm lens set to 15mm. The result was an approximately 90-degree angle of view, and it shows, too—not only do we see the baby but we see the large church looming in the background. I shot the second image with my 18–70mm lens set to 45mm, which resulted in an approximately 52-degree angle of view and a considerably diminished background church. In the third image, taken with my 70–300mm lens set to 135mm, resulted in an approximately 16-degree angle of view, and there the background is rendered as only out of focus tone and shape. Clearly, you get more of the story with the storytelling (wide-angle) lens, and when you want to isolate a subject from its surroundings to shoot a singular theme, you call upon the telephoto lens.

12–24mm lens at 15mm

You get more of the story with a wide-angle lens, and you isolate a subject from its surroundings with a telephoto lens.

18–70mm lens at 45mm

70–300mm lens at 135mm

SHUTTER
SPEED

INTERPRETING MOTION

Motion-filled photographic opportunities are present all around us—in our homes or on the street, in the office or at the park. Rare is the individual whose world is motionless. And it is in this very motion that photographic "gold" waits to be mined.

FREEZING ACTION

There is, perhaps, nothing more satisfying than a photograph that captures action frozen in crisp, sharp focus, allowing the viewer time scrutinize and analyze every nuance down to the smallest detail. You can return, time and time again, to savor that moment, frozen in time, long after that particular action has ceased.

The keys to recording great action shots are many, but at the top of that list is the use of the right shutter speed. For most outdoor action-filled shots, i.e. most sporting events, shutter speeds of 1/500 sec. or 1/1000 sec. are the norm. Your second consideration is your ISO choice, since the greater the ISO, the greater the likelihood of being able to use both small apertures and fast shutter speeds. Since focusing needs to be fast, the added depth of field provided by an aperture of f/16 or f/22 may come in handy if you aren't quite spot-on with your focusing.

In addition, the use of a motor-drive is essential. On a DSLR, the motor-drive is the auto-advance mechanism, which resets the mirror and shutter, enabling you to take the next shot without having to manually advance the shutter as you would with some film cameras. With most DSLRs, you have two auto-advance modes: continuous low and continuous high. Set the camera to the high mode, this way you'll be able

My daughter Chloe is convinced that sharks can come up the bathroom drain and eat her, so that's why we have to leave the bathroom door open when she bathes—so that we will better hear her cries for help when the shark arrives. Yet, she has no problem jumping into swimming pools around the world—despite their even bigger drains, as I have repeatedly pointed out to her.

Although it took some negotiating (the promise of ice cream later), Chloe indulged my desire to have her simply throw her wet head back several times as I attempted to freeze the action of her long hair and the water that was thrown off it. With ISO 400 and an aperture of f/11, I was able to record a correct exposure at 1/800 sec. Instructing her to stay in one spot and not move her feet when she come up from under the water, allowed me to prefocus, as well as to precompose, so that on the count of three, I was ready. And presto, this is the result!—an action-stopping, sharply focused image of "a day at the pool."

20–200mm lens at 100mm, f/11 for 1/800 sec.

to record the most images of the action before you. Then, since it's digital, you can quickly edit out the unsuccessful photos. With most action shots, the best one image is the result of taking a sequence of shots in which you anticipate when the action begins and when it ends, and begin to shoot just prior to the action's potential peak.

IMPLYING MOTION

Motion is everywhere, and when that motion is conveyed in photographs through the use of long shutter speeds, the results are often compelling as well as surprising. But one word of caution when shooting long exposures of subjects in motion digitally: noise! In addition to noise being a factor when using high ISOs, it is also a factor when shooting long exposures that last beyond 8 seconds.

If you can't find a pool, then you hope to at least get a chance to play in a fountain. My daughter Sophie, another water baby, is also the track-and-field star of the family. She has been running since birth! Asking her to jump over a small fountain would never enter your mind, since she will have already made half a dozen leaps by the time you've caught up with her.

Pointing my camera and 12–24mm lens up to the blue sky above the fountain, I set the shutter speed to 1/500 sec. and adjusted the aperture until f/8 indicated a correct exposure. I then recomposed the scene to capture this image of Sophie in flight.

12–24mm lens, 1/500 sec. at f/8

TIP CHECK YOUR EXPOSURES

If you're setting up to shoot an action scene, check the number of exposures left on your compact flash card. There's no worse feeling than firing the shutter release at the peak of the action only to discover that the camera recorded just a few frames and then quit because the card was full! Especially when staging the action, as with my shot of Chloe on page 54, I prefer to load an empty card into my camera. This is another reason why having three or four compact flash cards is a good idea.

There are numerous tunnels in and around the French and Swiss Alps, some of which extend for seventeen miles. I decided to take advantage of a motion-filled opportunity in one of them one day. With my camera set to Aperture Priority mode and my 18–70mm lens propped up on the dashboard, I set the aperture to *f*/8 and the autoexposure override to +1 and simply pressed the shutter release while I did my best to keep pace with the semi truck in front of me. The 22-second exposure resulted in a motion-filled scene—perhaps an image that could serve a useful purpose as a "Don't Drink and Drive" poster. But note the excessive noise, despite its being an effective image.

The Portland Rose Festival takes place every June along the banks of the Willamette River in Portland, Oregon. It is also one of the few festivals that affords the photographer a view from above as seen from the Morrison Bridge. With my camera and 12–24mm lens on a tripod, I set my aperture to *f*/11. When shooting at dusk, I *always* set my exposure from the dusky blue sky; so, with my camera pointed to the sky above, I adjusted my shutter speed until 4 seconds indicated a correct exposure. I then recomposed and shot the scene you see here. Note the relative absence of noise. That's because I used Kodak's Digital Gem Noise Reduction filter. This is a downloadable plug-in that you can order from Kodak's Web site. If an image needs noise reduction, I make it my last step in post-processing.

PANNING

Beyond the basic techniques of freezing action or implying it, there is panning. Another way to interpret motion, panning is when you move the hand-held camera parallel to a moving subject as it passes through your frame while depressing your shutter-release button. This ensures that your moving subject is rendered relatively stationary in a particular spot in your composition, while all of the actual stationary objects that surround the subject record as horizontal (or vertical, depending on you

pan) streaks. (Normally in panning compositions, the subjects are always moving right to left or left to right, for example a kid on a bicycle or a jogger, but you can expand your horizons and look for the *vertical* motion around you, for example the child on a pogo stick or a seesaw or a "free-fall" ride at the amusement park.)

To pan effectively, you will want to use shutter speeds of 1/60 or 1/30 sec., but again, since this is digital—with *no film costs*—you should also open yourself up to experimentation

and shoot at even slower shutter speeds, such as 1/4 and 1/8 sec. Depending on the lighting conditions when you pan, it may be necessary to use your polarizing filter, which will facilitate using these slower shutter speeds, since by its very nature the polarizing filter cuts the intensity of the light by two stops.

When you pan any subject, keep in mind that you *must have an appropriate background* in order to be successful. Backgrounds, when panned, are rendered as blurred streaks of color and tone, and the busier and more colorful the background, the better the panned subject will look. If you were to paint horizontal streaks onto a canvas in only one color,

the result would look like nothing more than a solid color with no evidence of streaking. But if were to use several colors, you would be able to distinguish the streaks.

In much the same way, panning a jogger against a solid blue wall will show little, if any, evidence of the panning technique because of the lack of tonal shift or contrast in the background. But if that same wall is covered with posters, it will provide an electrifying background when panned. Simply put, the greater the variety of color and contrast within the background, the more exciting the panned image will be. So, in addition to concentrating on the many panning opportunities, concentrate on the visual interest of the background.

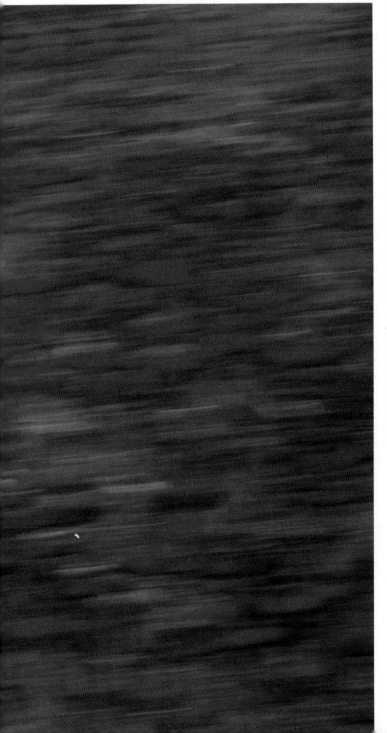

DIGITAL TECHNOLOGY & PANNING

I know of no other technique for interpreting motion that will make you count the blessings of the digital camera more than panning. It's a challenge to get panning right, and needless to say, a lot of shots are wasted until you get that one successful one. Panning has been a nightmare for film photographers due the high cost of film and processing. A student in one of my online courses informed me that "thanks to the lesson on panning," her husband went out and bought her a *digital* SLR after he noticed how much film from that one lesson went into the trash. Since she had six more weeks of lessons to go, he reasoned that she would probably be throwing away even more film and that "surely, the cost of all that film would more than pay for a new digital SLR."

And wouldn't you know it, when this story got out to the other class members, several of whom were also still using film, they made a point to place the garbage can right in front of their respective spouses and then do the "moan and groan"—"If only I had a digital camera...." By the time the class ended, there wasn't one film shooter in the bunch!

Besides lending themselves to obvious flower compositions, fields of flowers also provide great backdrops against which to pan. As my daughter ran through one such field in celebration of a long-awaited spring, I was quick to fire off numerous panning shots of her. With my aperture set to *f*/22, I was able to record a correct exposure at 1/40 sec. on this bright, overcast day.

35–70mm lens, f/22 for 1/40 sec.

PAINTING WITH SHUTTER SPEED

ntil recently, the following was the "rule" in photography: Keep the horizon line straight, and above all else, make sure it's in focus. It was also unthinkable for a photographer to deliberately handhold the camera (i.e., not use a tripod) at a very slow shutter speed. Those who did branch out from this norm were often scoffed at, because the resulting images were, of course, blurry and out of focus.

Fortunately, times have changed, and the idea of, what I call, "painting with a slow shutter speed" has been embraced by many photographers. But, unlike panning, which is already challenging enough, painting is a real hit-or-miss affair. Still, when everything does come together, it is truly rewarding. (Have you priced abstract art lately? Creating it yourself is not only cheaper, but since you "painted" it yourself, it's also that much more rewarding.)

Combining the foreground branch with an unassuming terrace in the background hardly produces the postcard shot you'd want to record in St. Tropez, France, but when you apply the *painting* motion technique, the subject quickly becomes a fine-art "abstract painting." While handholding my camera during exposure, I simply swung the camera in an upward diagonal motion. I made seven attempts at this scene, and this proved to be my personal favorite.

80–200mm zoom lens, f/22 for 1/4 sec.

Painting with shutter speed is a simple technique, really. The challenge is in finding the right subjects: those with lots of color, contrast, and sometimes pattern—and no people (a streaked effect in people is often interpreted as photographer error since seeing people in such an abstract way tends to make people uncomfortable). Once you feel you've found one, you simply set a correct exposure that will allow you to use a shutter speed of 1/4 or 1/2 sec., and then at the moment, you press the shutter release, twirl, arch, jiggle, or jerk the camera inward and up and down, or side to side, or round and round. And presto—an instant abstract painting!

Just as they were for Claude Monet with his brush and canvas, flower gardens are the number one subject of photographers for painting with shutter speed, but don't overlook other compositional patterns as well, such as marinas, fruit/vegetable markets, and even crowded stands at NFL games. Also, consider painting in low light, for which shutter speeds can range from 2 to 8 seconds—the difference is that you should make slower movements than the quick and hurried jiggles described previously. The result can mimic the effect of an artist using a palette knife to apply paint, as the exposure time builds up one layer upon another.

Primroses and crocuses are welcome signs of spring as they hold the promise of the warm and sunny days to come. Handholding my camera during the exposure, I simply made a circular movement as I aimed down at the bed of primroses. I was both surprised and delighted to discover that this circular motion recorded a "flock of flying and colorful seagulls." Experimentation can, and often does, prove successful, and again, digital photographers never have to fret over the film cost of these experiments—since there are none!

35–70mm lens, f/22 for 1/4 sec.

ZOOMING

How do you make a stationary subject "move"? You zoom it! With the proliferation of zoom lenses on the market today, I'm surprised that the zooming-during-exposure technique hasn't been revived.

It's a bit easier to create this effect with slower shutter speeds, such as 1/2 sec. or 1 second, since a slower shutter speed gives you a bit more time to zoom the lens during the exposure. Also, unless your subjects are in deep shade or low light, you will need a 3- or 4-stop neutral density (ND) filter to reduce the bright daylight coming into the lens. The addition of the ND filter will allow you to maintain a correct exposures at these slower shutter speeds.

Experience has taught me that it's best to begin any composition you want to zoom by framing it first with the widest

angle of any given zoom lens and then zooming toward the longer end. For example, if you're using a 17–35mm zoom lens, begin at 17mm and zoom to 35mm. With an 18–55mm lens, begin at 18mm and zoom to 55mm, and with a 70–300mm lens, begin at 70mm and zoom to 300mm. This effect *will* produce the desired results—but not without practice. Don't be disappointed if your first few attempts don't measure up. And remember the number one rule for all of us digital shooters: Every shot you take is "free," so fire away!

With my camera and 17–35mm lens on a tripod, I first made a straightforward composition of this warning sign in a shipyard. Then, with the addition of my polarizing filter (which caused a 2-stop loss in light), I set my aperture to *f/22* and got a correct exposure at 1/4 sec. As I pressed the shutter release, I zoomed the lens from 17mm to 35mm to record an explosive effect during this quick exposure.

17–35mm lens, f/22 for 1/4 sec.

TIP MAKE USE OF "CHIMPING"

Whether you are freezing action, implying motion, panning, painting, or zooming, make use of "chimping." In fact, the creative use of shutter speed that is often needed with motion-filled photography is one of the best excuses for chimping! And what is chimping? It is the viewing of the image you just shot right away in your camera's LCD.

Rumor has it that this whole idea of viewing what you shoot right away was given birth to last fall during an NFL game during which one of the professional sports photographers was seen chimping in between time-outs. He was editing/deleting those images that didn't make the grade from his compact flash card. The thought was that he might present his photo editor with a compact flash card that contained only his best work, which would, of course, be "cheating" in that it would give a false impression of what actually took place.

For anyone to even be concerned with this sounded like playground immaturity to me, unless there was a behind-the-scenes competition between several photographers for which every image, from the good to the bad to the downright ugly, needed to be accounted for. For me, editing as I go is the norm since it serves two useful purposes: (1) it frees up space on the compact flash card, and (2) it saves time in postprocessing since I've already deleted the obvious bad shots.

So, I'm here to announce that, short of a photographic competition in which I must account for all of my images, I embrace chimping with a zeal akin to drinking my Diet Pepsi—they are both behaviors I won't be giving up anytime soon. Having said that, and because the temptation to view your shots immediately is too much to resist, I would advise that you carry a fully charged spare battery with you in the field. If the actual photographing doesn't run your battery down, then surely the LCD viewing and in-camera editing will. And if you don't carry a spare battery, then purchase one of those 110-volt power adaptors that fits snuggly into the cigarette outlet of the car so that you can plug the battery in and charged it up without having to call it a day and return home quicker than you planned.

LIGHT

THE IMPORTANCE OF LIGHT

The importance of light can never be overstated. Without light, no one would be able to see anything. Theoretically, everyone would be blind. It is the first light of morning that assures most of us that the day has begun, and it is this same light that assures those individuals working the graveyard shift that their work day is about to come to a close. For most people, the proverbial "light at the end of the tunnel" means the end of a sorrowful or difficult period. Light does have a direct effect on people's emotions, easily affecting our moods. Almost everyone has had the blues, and this common type of depression is strongly associated with the winter season and its shorter amount of daylight.

Whether lighting is harsh, gentle, glaring, or diffused; whether it is cold or warm; whether it comes straight at us like a spotlight or from the side, behind, above, or below—it plays perhaps the greatest role in determining the *mood* of an image. When you photograph a stern-looking woman under diffused light, you temper her appearance. When you photograph a meek and soft-spoken teenage boy under harsh light, you can make him seem a bit cold and aloof. Both subjects would argue, "Hey, that's not me," upon seeing these photographs and for good reason. The quality of the light and the impression it creates are in direct contrast to the way the subjects define themselves. Similarly, your disappointing reaction to the close-up of the white rose in your garden is understandable, considering that the rose actually seems to be light blue. Such is the "color" of the light in open shade—blue. And such is the character of light—always changing, not always what it originally seems.

Another important aspect of light, which we'll cover more in a minute, is its direction. Do you remember, as a small child, when you visited the Haunted House during Halloween? As you rounded the corner in that creaky hallway, you suddenly saw someone who appeared quite ugly and frightening for that fraction of a second that he held a flashlight under his chin and shined it on his face. The fear was in large measure due to the light and its angle across the "monster's" face. Whether you photograph people or landscape, close-ups or abstract compositions, much of your image-making will probably involve some form of *directional light*: frontlight, sidelight, or backlight.

In addition, diffused light, a lighting condition embraced by experienced photographers, is akin to the light a studio photographer creates using soft boxes on electronic strobes, thereby causing the light to spread out evenly over the subject. Diffused outdoor lighting is ideal for shooting portraits, subjects in wooded areas, or close-ups of flowers.

And finally, all light—whether it's frontlight, sidelight, backlight, or diffused light—imparts a color cast onto the subject, depending on the time of day. Morning light is warmer than midday light, and late afternoon light (shortly before sunset) is even warmer still, whereas diffused light can at times be "blue."

Light plays, perhaps, the greatest role in determining the mood of an image.

The harbor of Marseille is one of the busiest in all of France. With my camera on a tripod, I was eager to shoot the many boats and houses as well as the distant fortress above the harbor—so eager, in fact, that I proceeded to shoot several images of the harbor knowing full well that at that moment a large cloud was moving across the sky and was blocking the sun. As you can clearly see, a blue color cast permeates the image (top). It's the direct result of the harbor being under the "umbrella" of a cloudy sky, which will always produce blue light.

Within minutes, however, the large cloud had moved on, and warm late-afternoon light flooded the scene. The difference is clear. Which of the two is more inviting? Obviously, the warmer image.

Top: 80–200mm lens, f/22 for 1/20 sec.
Bottom: 80–200mm lens, f/22 for 1/125 sec.

FRONTLIGHT

What is meant by *frontlight*? It's light that hits the front of your subject, as if your camera were a giant spotlight bathing everything in front of it in light. Of course your camera doesn't actually do this, but the sun sure can! For most of your picture-taking efforts, you should get in the habit of shooting subjects when they are frontlit, and also early in the morning or late in the afternoon when the sun is at a low angle to the horizon (and therefore not as harsh and unflattering as midday light). For some of us that means our sleep will be interrupted or our dinner will be delayed.

Failing to shoot when the sun is at low angles to the horizon will often spell disaster in your images for a variety of reasons, not the least of which is the absence of warm and flattering light. It doesn't take long for that giant "spotlight" of the sun to get high in the sky, and yet, in the times when many amateurs are out shooting—10:00 a.m. to 4:00 p.m. on any given clear summer day—the light is very harsh, without any real warmth, and it is famous for creating raccoon shadows under the eyes of your human subjects. Midday light, as it is called, should be reserved for sitting by the pool and working on your tan!

When experienced photographers speak enthusiastically about frontlight, they are most often referring to its color: the golden hues of morning light and the orange-golden hues of sunset. These colors bring warmth, passion, intensity, and sentiment to any subject, whether it is a person, an animal, or a landscape.

When photographers speak enthusiastically about frontlight, they are most often referring to its color: the golden hues of morning and the orange hues of sunset.

LIGHT: HUMAN EYE VS. CAMERA

The human eye can see light and dark simultaneously. In terms of camera stops, the human eye can see and register a range of 16 stops. Film cameras were known for being able to see only a 5-stop range, and the most current of SLR digital cameras can see only a 6-stop range. So what can you do when you want to record a range of light that's greater than 6 stops? Take several different exposures of the same composition—on a tripod, of course—and when you return home, "blend" them together in Photoshop (see page 146).

The low-angled frontlight in this image casts its warm glow across my wife, Kathy, in a field of poppies, accentuating her warm and inviting expression. With my camera on a monopod, I set the aperture to f/5.6, and because she was wearing white, I pointed the camera to the green field to her right to adjust my shutter speed until a -2/3 exposure was indicated. Metering for frontlit green at -2/3, will assure you of a correct exposure overall, even when white is a dominate part of the overall composition. (See pages 82–83 for more specifics on metering.)

80–200mm lens, f/5.6

SIDELIGHT

Sidelight hits one side of a subject, illuminating only part of it and leaving the other parts in "darkness." The subject takes on a three-dimensional quality due to the illusion of depth created by the contrast between light and dark. As a result, sidelight is often considered the most dramatic type of lighting. Subjects that are sidelit suggest mystery and intrigue, intimacy and sensuality, as well as deception and the underworld.

Both painters and photographers of the nude have made sidelight their number one choice, as the interaction of light and shadow reveals and defines the form of their subjects. Another classic use of sidelight has been perfected by Hollywood: sidelighting the criminal's face. This foreboding image can cause viewers to shiver at the unspeakable horrors that certainly must be lurking in the criminal's mind.

Sidelight is also responsible for bringing texture to the surface. A composition of rough hands or a wrinkled face is "felt" much more deeply when sidelit. And, not surprisingly, the optimal conditions for recording sidelit subjects are once again in the early morning or late afternoon.

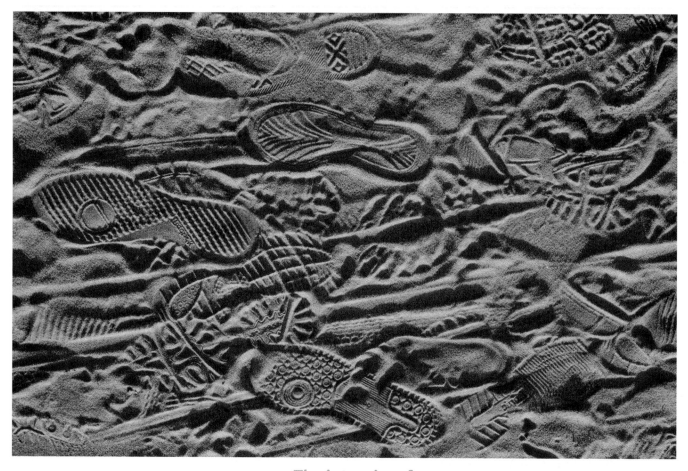

The intensity of texture is increased a hundredfold when that texture is sidelit. Something as simple as footprints in the sand along a shoreline take on a lifelike feeling when sidelit by the low-angled light of the setting sun. Another chief advantage to low-angled sidelight is that, unlike with low-angled frontlight, you don't have to worry about your long shadow getting in the way in the composition! For this shot, I placed my camera on a tripod, set my aperture to f/8, and let the camera set the shutter speed for me via Aperture Priority mode.

When I made this image, I was reminded of the saying, The reward is not in the planning of your journey, but knowing that you are now on your way.

18–70mm lens, f/8 for 1/180 sec.

The Rhine and the Moselle rivers of Germany are a castle lover's paradise, and the best time of day to shoot Castle Cochem on the Moselle river is late afternoon when it is sidelit. The resulting shadows and warm light create an image with depth and volume.

Arriving early one morning last fall, I was quickly disheartened to see such a strong veil of overcast light (top), but I was assured by the locals that this would dissipate by midday. When you find yourself confronted with "bad light," take advantage of the time to do your scouting. Bad light is great light for scouting, I have often said. I promptly set off hiking around the hillside vineyards, looking for preferred vantage points from which to shoot the castle should better light arrive later on that afternoon. And as luck would have it, the light returned and my hoped-for castle shot did happen—and, clearly, the warm light of late afternoon (bottom) is far more inviting than the much cooler, bluish composition taken earlier that morning. With my camera on a tripod, I metered off the vineyards behind the castle, adjusted my shutter speed until 1/100 sec. indicated a correct exposure, and then recomposed the shot you see here and shot several frames.

80–200mm lens, f/16 for 1/100 sec.

Subjects that are sidelit suggest mystery and intrigue, intimacy and sensuality, as well as deception and the underworld.

BACKLIGHT

If you're still not convinced that early morning and late afternoon provide the best light, perhaps I can still change your mind when it comes to backlight. It is backlight (when the light hits the back of your subject) that renders so many subjects as silhouettes. Backlight will always find you reaching for your sunglasses or, at the least, shading your eyes. Why? Because to shoot backlight, you must be facing the light source, and most often that means you are facing the sun itself.

Unlike sidelight, which conceals the subject in partial darkness, backlight can cloak the entire subject in total darkness. The resulting silhouetted shape—whether it's a tree, building, or person—is devoid of all details. This stripping away of a subject's individual characteristics might explain why many photographers prefer not to shoot silhouetted subjects. Without the details, the image is meaningless, or so the argument goes. I couldn't disagree more! Since silhouetting a subject *does* reduce it to but one element—shape—it's quite gratifying to showcase this shape against the backdrop of a sunrise or sunset. That lone oak tree on the horizon doesn't get its due until it is backlit against the early morning sunrise. The silhouetted couple on the beach in a warm embrace against the setting sun reminds all of us about love and romance. And because the couple is strictly rendered in the exposure as a shape, it is much easier to imagine that "that could be us."

Luck can play a big part of one's success in image-making, and as with the lottery, you can't win if you don't play. Although I had nothing in mind when I headed out the door to shoot the last hour of light and a hoped-for sunset, I knew that just being out "in it" I would find something. A roadside ditch of wild oats and various grasses, proved to be fertile ground for making this backlit image of a lone feather against the light of the setting sun. With my camera on a tripod, I set my aperture, and while metering in manual exposure mode, I pointed the camera to the left of the feather and adjusted the shutter speed off the backlit sky—without the sun in the frame—until 1/400 sec. indicated a correct exposure. I then recomposed and shot the image you see here.

70–300mm lens, f/5.6 for 1/400 sec.

TIP

THINK AHEAD

Whenever I shoot sunrises or sunsets, I always think about how I could use the image as a "digital sandwich" later and compose accordingly. This was certainly the case when I made the photo below, as you can see on page 122.

Who doesn't like silhouettes?

Backlight is the key, and when composed against a rising or setting sun, any object in front of the resulting strong backlight will surely be rendered as a silhouette—*if* you set the exposure for the bright background.

Contributing to the richness of this sunset image was the large amount of smoke in the air from area forest fires. The smoke was so thick in the air that no amount of filters or "Photoshopping" could have ever rendered such vivid colors. With my camera on a tripod, I set my aperture, took a meter reading from the bright sky to the left of the sun, adjusted my shutter speed until a correct exposure was indicated, and recomposed.

80–400mm lens, f/16 for 1/100 sec.

What about those times when the subject is backlit and you don't want to make a silhouette? When a subject has any degree of transparency, it can "glow" when backlit, rendering not only shape but, as in the case of dew-covered grasses, some wonderful textures, as well. When I stopped by the side of the road here, I was quickly immersed in a world of "jewel-laden" grasses and countless close-focus opportunities.

With my camera and 70–180mm Micro lens on a tripod, I set my aperture to *f*/11, adjusted my shutter speed until 1/125 sec. indicated a correct exposure, and fired off several frames. It was imperative, as it is when shooting most close-ups, that I choose a point of view parallel to the subject since depth of field becomes quite shallow when shooting close-ups.

70–180mm Micro lens, f/11 for 1/125 sec.

DIFFUSED LIGHT

Diffused light is soft, with subtle shadows. This illumination is much kinder to the face and evokes feelings of calm. It also minimizes wrinkles and other skin imperfections. (Of course, with Photoshop even small pimples or wrinkles are an easy fix, but the task of fixing these elements is much easier when they're photographed in frontlight or diffused light.) Diffused light is also the light of choice for many experienced nature photographers. The almost shadowless quality of diffused light makes exposures of waterfalls, for example, much easier due to the absence of contrast.

Nothing could be easier than determining exposure when you're working with diffused light. Whether you're shooting a portrait, a flower, or autumn leaves on the forest floor, every part of the image is uniformly lit. So, photographing scenes in diffused light is simply a matter of composing, focusing, and shooting. There are no bright highlights or dark shadows to confuse your light meter.

So that there's no confusion, however, diffused light is *not* identical to the light present when thick rain clouds fill the sky. Even though you can look up at the sky in diffused-light conditions, you should still be able to spot the sun behind the thin veil of clouds. If you look up at the sky and have no idea where the sun is, then you're shooting under the dark cloud of a threatening rainstorm.

Also, open shade is *not* diffused light either, but rather is nothing more than an area where the sun would normally shine but is presently being blocked by a building or a tree or some other object. Open shade is by far the bluest of light, as many unsuspecting wedding photographers have discovered. No bride likes to see herself in a blue wedding dress. This blue light contaminates everything—some things more severely than others—and most noticeably whites and light pastels. If you're still looking for an excuse to change from auto white balance to the Cloudy setting this would be the lighting condition in which to do it.

Part of an assignment I shot for a gold mining company in Mexico included making pictures of many of the children who attended a nearby school. The gold mine had donated quite a bit of money to the school for books and supplies, and had also paid for a new addition, and they wanted to call attention to this in their annual report to the stockholders. Eight large windows, on both sides of the schoolhouse, created some bright yet diffused light inside, and it made my job much easier since, once again, light levels were relatively even. With my camera on a tripod, and my aperture set to *f*/5.6, I just aimed, focused, and shot, letting Aperture Priority mode select the shutter speed.

80–200mm lens, f/5.6 for 1/60 sec.

If there's an outdoor market nearby and diffused light overhead, grab your camera gear and tripod and do some "shopping." Because of the color and truly showstopping patterns, outdoor markets continue to be a favorite haunt of mine. I swear some of the vendors at these markets have a degree in color theory or at the least have a graphic design background. How else can you explain their very graphic and colorful displays of arranged fruits and vegetables?

Oftentimes, I can travel very light when going to these markets, carrying just my camera and my 18–70mm f/2.8 Nikkor lens. The lens is wide enough for some shots, yet with its moderate telephoto end, I can just as easily come in tight on my subjects when closer cropping is called for. For the mound of strawberries above, I used a tripod and set my aperture to f/8. Since the light levels were even, I had no problem working in Aperture Priority mode, allowing the camera to set the shutter speed for me.

Another plus when shooting outdoor markets: Most if not all of the photographs you take are immediate contenders for your kitchen wall. If you're looking for some easy yet compelling imagery for the kitchen, outdoor markets are the place to go.

Above: 18–70mm lens, f/8 for 1/180 sec.
Left: 18–55mm lens, f/11 for 1/90 sec.

DUSK AND LOW LIGHT

As explained earlier, noise is normally associated with ISO—the higher the ISO, the more noise, or grain, appearing on the image. Short of using lower ISOs, there's no way around the noise problem. It is, for the time being, here to stay. (But, see pages 22–25 for some in-computer solutions to the noise problem.)

Noise goes hand in hand with picture quality. The more noise you record, the less sharpness there is in the image. Overall colors are affected, and the overall image looks like it has been pinpricked.

Another thing that creates noise is a long exposure time. There is a "breakdown" in the image sensor's ability to expose for long periods of time. For lack of a better description, it's as if the Pixel family is unable to "concentrate" long enough on the image that's flooding their house, and they quite simply fall apart and have a nervous breakdown. The result: noise.

And what do I mean by a *long exposure*? I've found that noise becomes quite apparent on exposure times that are longer than 8 seconds. For the most part, that should have minimal effect on most photographers, since most (whether shooting film or digital) are not inclined to shoot exposures as long as 8 seconds. The biggest reason for this is threefold: (1) a lack of motivation, since "there isn't that much to shoot in low light" (this is not true by the way); (2) uncertainty about how to set the exposure; and finally, (3) the need, in most situations, to use a tripod.

But, if you've been looking for a great excuse to use your camera in manual-exposure mode, try this: Grab your tripod, and stand outside your house at dusk, leaving just a few lights on inside. If you live in an apartment, just look around until you find a comparably illuminated subject. After deciding which lens to use—and regardless of what direction you're facing—anchor your camera to the tripod, set the aperture to $f/11$, and tilt the camera up to the dusky sky above the house, filling as much as 80 percent of the frame with sky. Adjust your shutter speed until the camera meter indicates a correct exposure, and then leave it alone. Recompose the scene of your house, and make take the shot. If my hunch is correct, this will be the start of many nights when you opt out of watching "must-see TV" for taking "must-shoot pictures" instead.

Just because there's no sky in this composition doesn't mean that I didn't use the sky to set my exposure to capture this view in Lyon, France. With my camera on a tripod, I set the focal length (35mm) and aperture (f/8 because "Who cares?" what aperture I use when everything is at the same focused distance—in this case, infinity), and then pointed the camera above the distant horizon into the dusky blue sky to meter. I adjusted the shutter speed until 4 seconds was indicated as the correct exposure and then recomposed. I tripped the shutter release with the camera's self-timer and shot several frames.

35–70mm lens at 35mm, f/8 for 4 seconds

Right near sunset, the last rays of light are joined with the first hints of the dusky, colored light to come. It is at this time of day that the quality of light is so magical that you will always come away with a compelling image—always! At dusk, both natural light and artificial light "are on the same page," so you needn't worry about blown out highlights. For example, in this image the two tungsten-bulb safety lights (which were at the top of a stairway on the deck of an oil tanker) and the sunset itself are the "same" exposure.

17–55mm lens, f/16 for 1/4 sec.

Beginning about fifteen minutes after sunset and lasting for only about ten minutes beyond that, the dusky blue sky will be the same exposure as a cityscape in front of it. After this short ten-minute window, the sky goes black, and this black sky is what most photographers end up shooting, as the numerous photo contest entries of "cityscapes at night" attest. The serious photographic downside to this time of night is in the compositional arena, as the dark sky doesn't offer up the much needed contrast/color separation between it and the other objects in the image. To see what I mean, take a look at these three images of Times Square in New York City.

The popularity of photographing this location is such that you'd be wise to stake your claim (i.e., a spot on the sidewalk) about thirty minutes before dusk. When the lights come on and the sky turns blue, you have several options. If you didn't bring your tripod, or you don't even own one, you can still easily get a handholdable exposure with ISO 640. The image above is an example of this: I handheld my camera and I pointed the camera to the dusky blue sky above the city to meter the scene. The resulting exposure "froze" the moving traffic. In addition, there is still a nice difference between the sky and the buildings.

It has been my preference, however, to shoot city scenes that capture all of the motion therein. This involves using the longest possible exposure times, and with the current digital technology and related noise factors, 8 seconds is about the maximum exposure time one can successfully record. This is certainly enough time—*if* you begin the exposure when the traffic is moving through the scene at its maximum capacity. So about five minutes after taking the image above, I placed my same camera and lens on a tripod, set my ISO and aperture, and again pointed the camera to the dusky blue sky above the city to meter. I adjusted my shutter speed until 4 seconds indicated a correct exposure, and then recomposed. As indicated by the line of red taillights, I was able to record the motion of the city traffic (opposite, top). I'm sure you'll notice that the sky in this exposure is a bit darker. That's because I "lost" a few minutes in setting up this shot after making the image above. But despite this loss of light in the sky, there is still enough contrast between it and the surrounding buildings, so those pesky mergers have been avoided.

Finally, as an example of why it's not a good idea to shoot city scenes after the short window of dusky blue sky has vanished, note the final exposure (opposite, bottom) taken ten minutes later. There is not nearly the same contrast between the buildings and the sky; in effect, there are now a number of "mergers" going on in this composition.

Above: 12–24mm lens, ISO 640, f/8 for 1/30 sec.
Opposite, top: 12–24mm lens, ISO 100, f/22 for 4 seconds
Opposite, bottom: 12–24mm lens, f/16 for 4 seconds

TAKING A METER READING

One of the most frequent questions in my on-location workshops is: How would you meter this? Regardless of subject, there never seems to be just one answer. Finding a subject seems to be the easy part for most shooters; not knowing *how* to take the meter reading seems to be the hard part.

The good news is that today's digital SLR is truly an amazing piece of machinery, and nowhere is this more evident than in the SLR's ability to meter a scene. Nikon continues to be at the forefront of this revolution, and it all started some years ago when the company introduced *matrix* metering. Matrix metering has become the standard in the digital industry, and it's all made possible by a computer chip.

In Nikon's case, a chip was programmed with more than a million different and correctly exposed pictures that were taken all over the world, outdoors and indoors, in every possible lighting and weather condition. The subject matter included close-ups, landscapes, abstracts, industrial shots, nature scenes, and, of course, people. So now, with your Nikon camera set in Matrix metering mode, you head out the door and frame up that red rose in your garden. With your macro lens in place, and because you want as much depth of field as possible, you have chosen an aperture of *f*/32. With the camera in Aperture Priority mode, you can allow the matrix metering to calculate the correct shutter speed, knowing full well that it has seen your rose before under these exact lighting conditions. And sure enough, if you check the LCD, you will see the perfectly exposed rose. Exposure has never been easier!

Does this mean that foolproof exposure has finally arrived? Not quite, and here are two reasons why this will probably never be the case: The first is that, as with any computer, there will always be the occasional "bug" in the system; in other words, there will always be some scenes that will fool matrix metering, and at these times, I resort to setting my exposure manually (see pages 84–85). The second, and perhaps most important, is that matrix metering has no idea when you want great depth of field or shallow depth of field, nor does it know if you want to imply motion, pan, or freeze action; these are decisions you must make. And most discerning pros make them with the camera in manual exposure mode.

So that there's no confusion, I'm not suggesting that, despite the advances made with digital SLRs, we all must resign ourselves to shooting in manual exposure mode. In fact, what I am suggesting is that we all can, for the most part, feel safe and secure when shooting in Aperture Priority mode. This is the mode to use when depth of field is an issue.

You can feel just as secure with your exposures when shooting in Shutter Priority mode for those times when shutter speed is your primary concern. I, like so many other seasoned professionals, have been scared to death by the promise of matrix metering. I had been shooting in manual exposure mode, using center-weighted metering for so long that anything else felt unsafe and unreliable; this, despite the claims made by matrix metering.

Only recently, over the course of the past six months, have I tested the waters of matrix metering. I've allowed myself the freedom of shooting in Aperture Priority mode, and I feel truly liberated by the results. I shot many of the images in this book in Aperture Priority mode, and that, for me, is one of the biggest photographic milestones I've ever crossed.

WHY NOT JUST USE AUTOEXPOSURE MODE?

I want to digress here for a just a moment and address one of the most common questions I get: Why not just shoot in the fully automatic exposure mode (better known as Program mode) and then quickly review the histogram on the camera's LCD monitor? The thinking being that if the histogram shows that the exposure is wrong, you can make some adjustments by using the + or – controls on the camera and shoot again.

Although the question is valid, it fails to take into account so many other variables that go into *the art of creative exposure*. First of all, in Program Mode there's no real control over depth of field or shutter speed. I'm fully aware of the latest offerings on some cameras, such as Program Landscape mode, Program Action mode, and Program Close-Up mode. These are, for all intents and purposes, nothing more than a narrow and preset exposure parameter for shooting some landscapes, some action-filled scenes, and some close-up scenes—but the key word here is *some*, not all!

Students who have fallen into the trap of shooting in these modes are quick to discover the lack of consistency in their exposures. The histogram is nothing more than a record of the quantitative value of the exposure relative to its highlights and shadows, and has nothing to do with the creative value of the exposure. Save yourself both time and trouble. Turn off the histogram, and if necessary, get a pair of reading glasses so that you can better see the creative exposure you're hoping for when you view the monitor.

The greatest gift you can give yourself in the exposure arena is teaching yourself how to use your camera in manual exposure mode and then calling upon manual exposure mode for those "difficult" exposures. Short of that, shooting in semiautomatic mode is a good idea as it saves time, but you should resign yourself to the Aperture Priority or Shutter

Priority modes only since either mode allows you to still retain full creativity over your exposures.

In addition, always shooting in autoexposure doesn't take into account another important element of image-making: what Henri Cartier-Bresson called the Decisive Moment. In the time you take to check your monitor, review the histogram, and make whatever adjustments you feel are necessary, the subject before you will have either turned away from the camera or moved on to another activity or disappeared. Imagine if that bull moose is now showing you its backside or your one-year-old daughter grows tired of taking her first steps and sits down to play with a toy, or the bee that was pollinating the very flower you focused on has since moved on to another. All of these Decisive Moments are now gone.

How is your histogram going to help you in situations of strong backlight and action? It can't! If you blow this difficult exposure, what are you going to do? Ask the kids (whom you don't know) to run through the fountain again in the exact same way they did when you tried to get the exposure right the first time?

Learning how to "read" difficult exposures is the most logical step, and when metering backlight for a silhouette effect, I always take my meter reading—in manual—from the sky to the left of, the right of, or above the sun. After setting my aperture and taking my meter reading from the sky to the right of the sun (while handholding the camera), I adjusted my shutter speed and, over the course of the next five minutes, made a number of frames of these kids playing tag in a fountain.

12–24mm lens, f/16 for 1/320 sec.

BACKLIT PORTRAITS

've begun to embrace and trust Nikon's matrix metering with a greater fervor than ever before. As you may have noticed, and as I mentioned on page 82, some of the images in this book were shot in Aperture Priority mode (I picked the aperture and the camera/light meter picked the shutter speed). But even though my dependence on manual metering has lessened, I still find that it is necessary to meter in manual exposure mode when I am presented with "difficult" exposures.

These exposures are not difficult because I couldn't decide how much or how little depth of field I needed, or because I couldn't decide if I should freeze or imply motion, but rather, they were difficult because of the *light*! Sometimes, despite matrix or five-point metering, the light meter will still be fooled and render an exposure that's either too light or too dark. Here again, Photoshop can help when you really blow an exposure, but again, I have to ask myself, Why not get it right in camera rather than spend all the time needed to correct it in Photoshop?

A classic example of a "difficult" exposure is the backlit portrait. Shooting backlit portraits can produce some powerful and emotion-filled imagery *if* you know where to take your meter reading *and* you use a reflector. The warm light that often illuminates the edges of the hair when a person is backlit creates a warm and healthy appearance. You must shoot outdoor backlit portraits when the sun is at a low angle in the sky, either early morning or late afternoon. As you frame up a backlit portrait, there's a danger in the light meter being fooled by the excessively bright rim light around the hair, which can cause a false meter reading.

*T*he warm light that often illuminates the edges of the hair in a backlit portrait creates a warm and healthy appearance.

As you can see in the first example (top), with the camera again set on Aperture Priority mode and my aperture set to f/5.6, the meter produced an exposure (1/500 sec.) that proved to be okay for the backlight but not for the face itself, which is rendered about two stops too dark. Granted, since I was shooting in raw mode, I could just as easily have added two stops of light to the face in postprocessing, but I would have had to use the Marquee tool in Photoshop, making certain that only the face was the "live" area so that when I brought its exposure up two stops I didn't overexpose the rim-lit hair another two stops. The time spent in Photoshop to make this correction would have been about ten minutes at least. Why not opt instead to use a reflector?

I sometimes use a reflector with backlit subjects, and this is particularly true for backlit portraits. A reflector is a circular piece of highly reflective fabric stretched tightly over a collapsible metal ring. The fabric is either shiny gold, shiny silver, or a sheer white material. Sizes can range from twelve inches in diameter to up to three feet. When pointed toward the light source (the sun in most outdoor cases), the reflector acts likes a dull mirror, reflecting back much of the light onto the subject. In this case, my wife held an eighteen-inch reflector with its gold foil side facing the western sky and sun (bottom). Gold light was then "bounced" onto her face. With my camera still set to the original exposure, I shot an additional exposure, and as you can see, the added fill light from the reflector made the exposure for the face correct (opposite).

All photos: f/5.6 for 1/500 sec.

BACKLIT NATURE SUBJECTS

For backlit flowers, I'll sometimes use a reflector. Without it, it's a challenge to get both the petals and the center of a backlit flower acceptably exposed. For backlit landscapes, I'll often rely on my graduated neutral-density filter. No camera on the market today can record, within a single exposure, the vast range of light and dark that exists within a backlit scene. In the "old days," photographers just had to grin and bear it, knowing full well that the happy medium of overexposing the backlight in order to bring up the foreground darkness was the best they could do.

Then someone had the brilliant idea to make a filter that, when placed over the front of the lens, would reduce the exposure of *just the backlit sky* by several stops, making the exposure for the backlit area much closer to that of the foreground area. The rest is history and graduated neutral-density filters have been around for at least ten years now. Despite Photoshop's promise of being able to correct the backlit exposure situation I've just described, I still subscribe to the belief that if I can correct something in camera, I will—since it will save me time!

Without the reflector here, I was able to get an acceptable exposure for the petals since petals themselves are somewhat transparent, but note the dark center of the flower. It's dark simply because it isn't transparent, and the exposure time required for it would be much longer than the time needed for the backlit petals.

The solution was to place some fill light onto the with my gold reflector. Holding the reflector up and out of camera range, of course, I was able to reflect much-needed sunlight back onto the dark center of the flower, and presto, the difference is clear.

Both photos: 80–200mm lens, f/8 for 1/200 sec.

Without graduated neutral-density filter

What do you do when you set an exposure for a backlit landscape and you *don't* want the foreground to go excessively dark? You reach for your graduated neutral-density filter. With my camera on a tripod, I chose a low viewpoint to convey the texture on the sandy beach, and since I wanted this to be a storytelling image (one with lots of detail/focus throughout), I set the aperture to *f*/22. To meter, I pointed the camera down toward the sand and adjusted the shutter speed until the meter indicated that 1/8 sec. was a correct exposure. I then recomposed to include the setting sun. When I did this, the meter indicated a correct shutter speed of 1/125 sec., but I ignored that reading and instead placed a four-stop graduated neutral-density filter on the lens. I slid the filter down into the holder on the front of my lens until the area of density was covering the section of the image from the top of the frame to the horizon line.

All I had to do was fire the shutter release (at *f*/22 for 1/8 sec.), and I knew I would record a correct exposure for the foreground as well as for the distant sun and horizon. Without the filter, the sun and sky are blown out.

12–24mm lens, f/22 for 1/8 sec.

With graduated neutral-density filter

SOMETIMES PHOTOSHOP *CAN* HELP

Photoshop *can* come into play very effectively when you are faced with extreme exposure differences for which no amount of exposure know-how will save the day. For example, Photoshop can do a great job of acting like a graduated neutral-density filter, or it can come to the rescue when you want to record detail in both the shadows and the highlights. (See pages 146–147 for more on this.)

COMPOSITION

FILLING THE FRAME

There may come a day, when setting a creatively correct exposure is all done by the camera, but I can't ever imagine there will come a time when a camera will be able to tell you what the best point of view is. There are two constants in the art of image-making: "seeing" and composition. And no amount of technology will replace either. The good news is that you can learn both the art of composition and how to "see."

Photographic composition is based, in part, on order and structure. Every great image owes much of its success to the way it is composed, which is, in essence, the way the elements are arranged. As with any good story or song, several elements are involved in the process of putting together a compelling composition. You can make your primary subject appear small and distant against the drama of its surroundings. You can opt to fill the frame, edge to edge and top to bottom with only the faces in the crowd at a football game or with only that box of cherries at the produce stand. You can compose to include a background that complements the subject or, alternatively, that contrasts with it. You can change your point of view, shoot-

ing on your hands and knees or from above. You can choose a horizontal, a vertical, or even a diagonal format.

In addition, you can utilize two specific characteristics that dominate every successful composition: tension and balance. *Tension*, which is the interaction of the picture elements, affects the viewer's emotions. *Balance* organizes the visual elements and keeps the viewer from tripping over the photograph's intent or meaning.

This brings me to the simplest composition tip: Fill the frame. If you're not a fan of landscapes but prefer the often hidden details of life, or you love taking pictures of people, the number one problem that may plague you and your approach to the final composition is an inability to fill your frame with

the subject. I liken this to buying a cup of coffee. You expect to get a full cup. And should you only get a cup that's half full, you feel cheated. The viewer may feel the same way when looking at your photographs. All that empty space around your subject makes the viewer feel that something is missing. And something *is* missing—it's called impact!

If you don't want your images to get the people's attention, then do the following: Stand further back from your subject, don't focus as close as you can, don't zoom out your telephoto lens as much as possible, and whatever you do, don't ever drop to your knees when shooting storytelling landscapes. If, on the other hand, you do want to create frame-filling images with impact, then do just the opposite.

In my composition class, I have each student choose a subject that's familiar to everyone—a person, a ball, a coffee cup, a flower, etc.—and then I instruct them to fill the frame with it. It's a simple yet surprisingly revealing exercise. Filling the frame reveals just how easy it is to achieve impact. Take the image here. It may not be a common thought to crop off a person's forehead or ears when shooting a "portrait," but creative imagery has never been about common thought. As my daughter Chloe sat on the couch, I came up behind her with my camera (set to Aperture Priority mode) and asked her to look up at me while I made several exposures.

70–180mm Micro Nikkor lens at 100mm, f/5.6 for 1/90 sec.

TIP **MAKE USE OF THE LCD**

Let's face it, if your DSLR camera didn't have that monitor on the back, would you really have bought it? It's the instant feedback of this tiny LCD that has ignited, and reignited, the passion of so many shooters today. Yet, despite this mother of all inventions, many photographers still fail to reach compositional success and create pictures with *impact*.

The solution? Use the LCD to check yourself. If the goal is to get closer, especially when shooting portraits (both formal and informal), fill the frame "all the way to the brim," as it were. Make sure you take at least one exposure in which you cut off part of the subject's forehead and perhaps even the ears. Then, look in the LCD monitor to check that you have indeed gotten close enough to achieve the impact you're looking for. When you compare a tighter composition with one that's not so close, more often than not the closer shot is the one you will prefer.

Empty space around your subject makes the viewer feel that something is missing.

Which of these two images would you rather display on your wall? If you're like most people, you'd choose the top image. It's simply more fulfilling. All of us, when given a choice, would take that front-row seat at the play, since it holds the promise of seeing and hearing *everything*.

After composing and taking you picture, look at the LCD monitor and ask yourself, When I share this with my friends will they feel like they have a front-row seat or one in the back of the balcony from which they have to strain to see what's going on? As a general rule, if your subject isn't touching or at least coming very close to touching the edges of the LCD, you have chosen to seat your audience in the balcony.

LEARNING HOW TO FILL THE FRAME

One of the best exercises for overcoming the inability to fill the frame is to grab your camera and tripod, and go out and shoot nothing but letters and numbers for a whole week. A couple of things will happen as you do this: (1) You will "see" letters and numbers that you never noticed before, which will undoubtedly lead to the discovery of other subjects you never noticed before either; the old saying "one thing leads to another" is true. And (2), in your attempts to fill the frame with that one number or letter, you will discover all the ways of getting closer: switching lenses, walking closer, lying down, or climbing stairs, for example.

Make it a point to shoot only letters or numbers with great character and color. And make sure you fill the frame with them. Where do you begin your search? Antique stores are great haunts, as are junkyards; so are old signs, possibly graffiti, harbors (filled with boat names), and even industrial yards.

You may find that you seek out some letters or numbers more than others. The letter K had always been a favorite with George Eastman. He said, The letter K seems to be such a strong and incisive sort of letter. Not surprisingly, the name *Kodak* was derived by trying out a number of combinations of letters to make words starting and ending with K.

When an old rusty scale in a junkyard got my attention, I set up my tripod and photographed all the numbers on it one by one. The 4 was my favorite, and perhaps I share the sentiments of George Eastman, as I found it to be a strong and incisive number.

Nearby in this same junkyard, I came upon a rusty old license plate and was soon filling the frame with a proud, ever stable letter H.

One of my recent and favorite finds was this letter S, which was part of a City of San Francisco water meter cover in the middle of a parking lot. I wasted no time in framing a composition that not only included the S, but the curving lines above and below it, which created interesting horizontal divisions.

Left: 70–180mm lens, f/11 for 1/200 sec.
Center: 70–180mm lens, f/11 for 1/320 sec.
Right: 70–180mm lens, f/11 for 1/45 sec.

I was quick to spot a single corn stalk leaning against a wooden post at a local fruit and vegetable stand in Vermont. While the frame may, at first glance, appear to be filled with the corn (above), it becomes clear that it's not filled as much as it could have been when compared with the second version (right). It doesn't take much to fill the frame, quite honestly. More often than not, it simply means walking a few inches closer or zooming your lens out to a longer focal length, and the rewards for making such a small stride can often be huge.

Both photos: 70–180mm Nikkor Micro lens, f/11 for 1/30 sec.

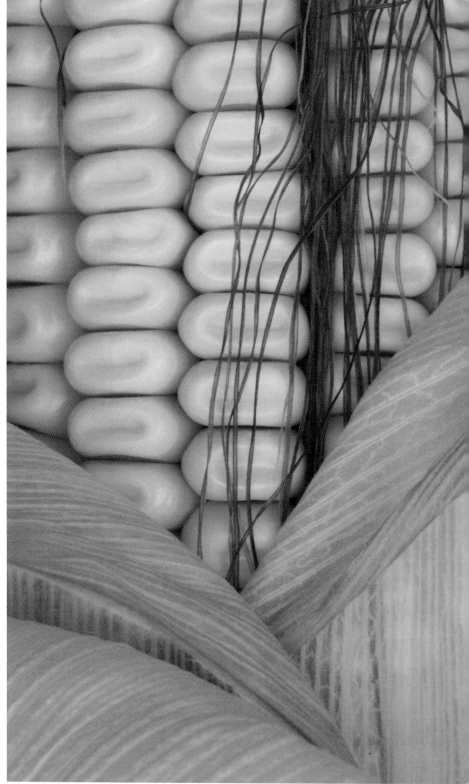

Learning to see line, texture, shape/form, pattern, and color can go a long way toward developing an awareness of the wealth of photographic opportunity around you. I often have my students just focus on either texture or pattern, which is a good way to discover both how easy and how important it is to fill the frame. Whether you choose to focus on texture or pattern, make a point to "carry that message" to all four corners of the image. This kind of imagery is compelling, independent of the subject itself, and the reason is simple: It is effective composition.

Downtown Tampa offers up a wealth of photographic material when it comes to line, shape, texture, pattern, and color. This sculpture is a good example of both line and pattern. I used a tripod, selected Aperture Priority mode, and chose f/32 for maximum depth of field—after I had first found a composition that truly filled the frame.

70–200mm lens, f/32 for 1/15 sec.

BACKGROUNDS

Over the past three years, I've had the pleasure of critiquing over ten thousand photos taken by students in my online courses at BetterPhoto.com. Each week, the students upload their results to the Web site, and I critique their top three images for that week's lesson. Although the task of critiquing more than two hundred images every week may seem daunting, it has actually been both inspiring and revealing. Each week, without fail, I get to see some truly outstanding photographs—photographs that make me laugh, smile, and sometimes even cry, photographs that make me stop, look, and feel!

Although I wish this were the norm with every image I critique, unfortunately, it's not. Many of the images fall short of their goal, and well they should, since the shooters are students, after all. And, if the images don't fall short because the subject doesn't fill the frame well, it's due to the second most common composition problem: a distracting background.

A detective will say, What about his background? An employer will say, Tell me about your previous employment. A doctor will say, Tell me your medical history. Background "checks" are the norm in everyday life—except in marriage and photographic composition! How many couples would

The circled flower (far left) shows my subject in its surroundings. Note the wonderful, dark open shade in the background (where the arrow points); since I would be exposing for the flower in sunlight, I knew that shade would be rendered easily as black, providing a nice contrast with the flower.

But, for my first attempt, in my haste I inadvertently divided the frame in two with the black shade and the gray sidewalk (left). There's nothing more confusing to the eye than a 50/50 split. Plus, the bit of surrounding foliage contributes to the busy, distracting background. In this case one problem (a failure to fill the frame with the main subject) led to another (an unsuccessful, cluttered background). After slowing down and really looking at the viewfinder, I got in close and made a minor shift in my point of view (tilting the camera up a bit to eliminate the gray sidewalk).

Below: 80–200mm lens, f/5.6 for 1/320 sec.

even make it to the alter if one or the other spouse first has a thorough background check? Oh yes, I forgot, love is blind, and that same blindness is what prevents so many photographers from recording some really great images.

Amateur photographers are often so taken by what they see inside the viewfinder and so blinded by their passion for their main subject that they fail to look at—let alone think about—what's going on in the background of their composition. They cannot see the problems with the background, even when they look in the LCD screen—and even after processing the image on the computer.

What causes background trouble? Several things. At times it can be the wrong aperture (resulting in too much depth of field), not paying attention to light (resulting in too much contrast between light and dark), the wrong point of view (resulting in that telephone pole sticking out of your daughter's head). And then there are those jarring tones or shapes in the background that are in disturbing contrast to the focused subject (for example, that out-of-focus background of purple flowers makes for a disturbing tonal contrast behind the bright red tulip). Pay attention to the backgrounds of your compositions before making the exposure.

If you want to show your friends that vacation photo of your daughter having fun in the French Alps, it makes perfect sense to include the swing set, the ground, and the distant mountains. But, if you want to create an illusion of space, distance, and possible danger, simply change your point of view and move in much closer with the same lens and shoot *only* the subject at the peak of the upswing against *only* the mountains in the background. Handholding my camera (yes, I do on occasion shoot without a tripod!), I set my aperture to *f*/11 and adjusted my shutter speed until 1/320 sec. was indicated as the correct exposure.

Since this road trip was made without Mom, I was in for some explaining when I later shared this image with my wife. My reasoning for taking many of my "before" shots is to help my students "see"; but in this case, the before shot also helped my wife see that, at no time, was our daughter in any danger.

Left: 12–24mm lens, f/11 for 1/320 sec.

DELIBERATE "MERGERS"

In some situations, you'll want to deliberately merge separate elements, sometimes for humor, other times for abstraction. The goal of a successful "merger" is to cause a momentary sense of disorientation.

During a break in a commercial assignment, the art director, Edward, and I took a walk around a portion of Lake Geneva in Switzerland. The famous fountain in the lake was soon the center of my attention as I asked Edward to pose for the camera with his lips pursed, so as to suggest that he was blowing a stream of water out of his mouth. With my camera on a tripod, I fired off several frames while shooting in Aperture Priority mode.

80–200mm lens, f/22 for 1/30 sec.

The Tour Rose is one of the more famous, yet hidden, landmarks in Lyon, France. By day it is open to the public, but right after sunset it becomes private property. I always wanted to shoot the Tour Rose at night but never had the courage to ask the resident who owned the terrace that afforded the best view of the Tour Rose. In fact, there was a well-marked sign, right at the entrance to the property that read, in effect, Don't ask about taking pictures from my terrace, and yes, even I can be intimidated. But after sharing my longing to shoot the tower at dusk with an acquaintance, I was informed the next day that "it was all arranged."

The following evening I was quickly immersed in framing a number of compositions. Since this would probably be my only opportunity to photograph the tower from this vantage point, I was both excited and nervous—and it showed. Initially, a number of my compositions suffered from "mergers" due to my point of view and lens choice. Note how the foreground lamppost merges with the background tower above. I tried moving left and right, but only when I moved in closer, tilted the camera up, and changed the focal length from 28mm to 20mm did I finally achieve the separation I wanted between the background and the foreground. In both examples, the exposures are the same: f/16 for 2 seconds, on a tripod, of course. I took my meter reading from the dusky blue sky above.

Above: 17–55mm lens at 28mm, f/16 for 2 seconds
Opposite: 17–55mm lens at 20mm, f/16 for 2 seconds

THE RULE OF THIRDS

In sports, a game is never allowed to end in a tie. Football, basketball, baseball, tennis, soccer, and golf all must declare a winner, so periods of overtime or extra innings, etc., are played until someone can finally be declared the winner. Why is this? It has everything to do with the indecision and the tension that indecision creates. Bottom line: Someone needs to be declared the winner before the brain can relax.

In photographs, the eye responds to compositions that are divided in half in much the same way. The eye can clearly see and, subsequently, feel the indecision in an image that is one half sky and one half landscape, or what is called a 50/50 composition. The eye feels this negative tension and is quick to respond with an unfavorable reaction. It demands that a "winner" be declared.

The ancient Greeks were the first to become aware of this psychological phenomenon and soon developed a proven method of artistic composition known as the Greek Mean. In its simplest form, the Greek Mean—also known in the art world as the Rule of Thirds—advocates dividing the compositional area of an image into thirds, both horizontally and vertically, to aid in subject placement. In landscape compositions, this often means that there's a deliberate placement of the horizon line near the top or bottom third of the image. As a general rule, if interest is greatest above the horizon line, then the horizon line should appear near the bottom third, and if interest is greatest below the horizon line, the horizon should fall near the top third. In effect, the visual weight of either composition makes it obvious that there is a "winner" between the sky above or the landscape below.

One of the most surprising, yet most welcome and overdue, features found on some DSLR cameras is the *compositional grid* that can be made to appear in the viewfinder with the press of a button. It is, in every respect, a Rule of Thirds grid. Not all cameras have this feature, but if yours does, you should leave it switched on permanently. This grid can be a tremendous help in creating compelling compositions, in particular with landscapes and cityscapes, helping you align the horizon near the top or bottom third of the frame, and keeping it straight. If you don't have the grid feature, try to imagine it there in your viewfinder or see the tip at right. Either way, keeping the grid in mind will definitely help improve your compositions.

Oregon has, without a doubt, some of the most beautiful coastlines in all the world. Despite its well-deserved reputation for rain, its coastline is one subject that has never disappointed me, rain or shine. Oftentimes, I've been very fortunate to find myself shooting coastal sunsets where only remnants of that day's rain clouds remain. These remnants often lead to some wonderful and compelling skies.

Since I wanted to emphasize the sky on this particular evening, I made a deliberate choice to place the horizon line near the bottom third of the frame. There's no mistaking that the subject here is the sky, since it dominates the composition. With my camera on a tripod and my aperture set to $f/16$, I simply adjusted the shutter speed until the camera's meter indicated that 1/160 sec. was the correct exposure for the strong backlight.

12–24mm lens, f/16 for 1/160 sec.

From atop a nearby dike, I was able to shoot down on this large field of tulips, and because I felt interest was greatest below the horizon, I chose to place the horizon line near the top third of the frame. With my camera on a tripod, I set my aperture to $f/32$ and adjusted my shutter speed to 1/30 sec. for the early morning frontlight falling on the scene before me.

80–200mm lens, f/32 for 1/30 sec.

TIP — MAKE YOUR OWN RULE OF THIRDS GRID

If your camera doesn't have the compositional grid feature, not to worry. If you still have the transparent plastic cover that protects the LCD you can take a Sharpie pen and draw a Rule of Thirds grid on the cover using a small straight edge to get the lines level. Simply draw two evenly spaced horizontal lines and two evenly spaced vertical lines, dividing the area into nine equal spaces.

If you don't have this LCD cover anymore, try a piece of 2-inch wide clear packing tape. Cut a piece a bit longer than the monitor, draw the grid on it, place it on the monitor, and you're in business.

HORIZONTAL VS. VERTICAL

'm fond of my students asking me, When is the best time to shoot a vertical? My answer is always the same: Right after you finish shooting the horizontal! Photoshop does a great job of cropping images, but when you crop into any image—and especially when you crop a vertical from a horizontal—image degradation is often *huge*. The new composition may work out just fine for a 5 x 7-inch print for your home office, but it will never hold up when printing at much larger sizes—and it certainly won't survive as a commercially viable stock photograph, since its file size is now way too small. At the risk of sounding like a broken record, get the job done right *in camera*—this applies to all subjects and all compositional arrangements. So, always shoot both horizontal *and* vertical compositions.

The best time to shoot a vertical composition is right after you've made the horizontal one. Scratch that. The *only* time to shoot a vertical is right after the horizontal. Attempting to crop this horizontal image of my wife into a vertical one would have not only meant time wasted on the computer, but it would have resulted in a lower print quality, as well, which is hardly flattering to the subject. It is such an easy thing to add to your "checklist" of things to remember when you're out and about shooting images.

Above: 200–400mm lens at 200mm, f/5.6 for 1/320 sec.
Opposite: 200–400mm lens at 300mm, f/5.6 for 1/320 sec.

WORKING YOUR SUBJECT

*W**orking your subject* is an oft-spoken term in many of my workshops. As we've been talking about here, students are often quick to move on to something else before having really explored the many possibilities of the scene they've just photographed. They don't explore different points of view, different lens choices, and of course, different formats (i.e., vertical *and* horizontal). Stay with your subject for a while. It will pay off.

Following a long day of picking up scrap lumber around my brother's recently constructed house, we began the bonfire. Over the course of the next two hours, my brother and I and several friends sat around the fire just shooting the breeze. At some point, my eyes caught sight of my brother's hands and coffee cup, and I felt it would make a nice image when photographed against the backdrop of the fire. The inclusion of his heavy shirt cuffs, coupled with the cup of coffee and fire, serves as a strong indication that this was no summertime bonfire but, obviously, a cold winter's day (above). I used a tripod for both images and waited for about thirty minutes until the once-roaring fire slowed to burning embers to get the second shot (right).

Both photos: 80–200mm lens at 200mm, f/8 for 1/60 sec.

PICTURE IN PICTURE

More often than not, *every* picture has another equally compelling image inside it, even if getting to that compelling image means using macro or close-focusing equipment. Train your eye to see these other images, *before* you leave the scene before you.

Most of my students don't see these other images until it's too late. Pulling that other image out via cropping with Photoshop is not an option, due to the subsequent image degradation that will result. Learning to see that other image (and then cropping) *in camera* via a different lens choice or focal length will most often do the trick of recording that other compelling image that lays in wait.

At the local fish market in Dubai, a flurry of activity takes place every morning, seven days a week. Fish are bought and sold, literally, by the thousands, and they are then rushed off to the many restaurants where they will be served up fresh. Although I was quite happy to frame this fish vendor with a distant mosque in the background, I also felt that just a shot of the basket of fish would make for a nice image. I simply zoomed my lens from 100mm to 400mm to frame just the wire basket full of fish. Since I chose a slightly higher point of view for the second shot, I was able to use the large blue storage bins where the fish were kept as a great background of color and tone against which to contrast the bright fish.

Right: 80–400mm lens at 100mm, f/5.6 for 1/800 sec.
Below: 80–400mm lens at 400mm, f/5.6 for 1/800 sec.

SCALE AND THE LANDSCAPE

The human shape is perhaps the most unmistakable shape in all the world. As a result, when you include it shape in any large and expansive landscape, an obvious sense of scope and scale results. This happens regardless of whether that landscape is a nature scene or something more urban or industrial. But I often tell my many nature landscape students that if they one day hope to make money with their camera, they would be wise, whenever possible, to shoot another exposure with a lone figure in that same landscape. It's a fact that images that include a person in the landscape, more often than not, have a higher market value than those that don't.

The train station next to Lyon's Satolas Airport has been honored with numerous architectural and design awards, and for very good reason. With its wide and sweeping design, the interior can be further magnified by the use of a wide-angle lens. It's also flooded with daylight, making handheld exposures quite easy. To illustrate the importance of the human form in this image, take your finger and simply cover up the woman; then note how the size and scale of the train station is not nearly as apparent.

12–24mm lens, f/8 for 1/320 sec.

Shortly after sunset, the light in the shipyards and the light in the sky are of the same exposure value. As I was working from a nearby guard shack rooftop, my assistant radioed the two dock worker's below, guiding them into position near the bow of the boat. Their presence was important primarily for one reason: to bring a sense of scale to this very large container ship. With my camera on a tripod, I set my aperture to *f*/16, pointed the camera to the sky above the ship, adjusted my shutter speed to 1/2 sec., and then recomposed the scene you see here and fired off several frames. Again, block out these two shapes with your finger and the size and scope of this ship are not communicated nearly as well.

80–200mm lens, f/16 for 1/2 sec.

WHITE BACKGROUNDS:
AN EXERCISE IN COMPOSITION

Let me share with you an exercise that will not only make you more attentive to composition but will also provide endless hours of shooting fun: photographing objects against a plain background of white Plexiglas (the type used on light tables). It's a particularly handy exercise if you're unable to get outside as often as you'd like or if you live in an area where inclement weather dampens your enthusiasm about heading outdoors.

For my setup, I use two monolights called Alien Bees (model #B1600) from the great folks at White Lightning. Both of these flashes are wrapped in a Velcro enclosure called a soft box. Like its name implies, the soft box "converts" the light emitted by the monolight from harsh light to *soft* light.

For this kind of photography I set my exposure for the two flashes at around the "Who cares?" aperture of $f/11$ since I shoot straight down on almost everything. With my flash meter set to $f/11$, I turn on the top flash and adjust the flash output until I record a reading of $f/11$. I then turn this unit off and turn on the other flash, and again, adjust the flash output until I get a reading of $f/11$. After this, I turn both units on, and with my aperture set to $f/11$, I begin to set up any number of subjects on the 2 x 3-foot piece of Plexiglas, which I lay on top of the bottom soft box.

Suffice it to say the sky's the limit here when it comes to choosing what to shoot on this shadow-free, pure white lighting setup. Flowers, fruits, and veggies are obvious choices and worth your time, for sure, but think about *all* the other possibilities. When you aren't worrying about the background, you are free to focus on the composition and the placement of whatever objects you're using.

Both my lights (the smaller, top one and the larger, bottom one on the floor under the piece of Plexiglas) emit the same amount of flash at the same amount of time via the built in slave unit on each flash head. I use the flash sync cord from the smaller flash (the top one) so that when I fire the shutter release, the slave from the other flash "sees" the flash and then fires at the same time. This all happens at 1/250 sec., a bit too fast for the human eye to see.

When you buy a bouquet of flowers to liven up a room, they are usually dead within a week. Why not immortalize them in a photographic composition of color and pattern? After purchasing a bouquet of carnations, I quickly clipped the stems of each one and placed them in a deliberate pattern on the white frosted Plexiglas. I set the aperture to *f*/11 based on the flash meter's exposure information and made a number of compositions, shooting straight down on the arrangement. Rather than sitting on a table in a vase, these carnations are now immortalized forever, hanging on a wall.

35–70mm lens, f/11 for 1/250 sec.

When a glass jar or bottle falls to the floor and breaks into a million pieces, it immediately evokes some strong, emotional responses: Oh, &*#!*&#! As one who has done his share of dropping, as well as cleaning up, I have often wished I could photograph these spills in the purest way. Only recently did it occur to me that I could easily re-create the spills by dropping a glass jar or bottle from a distance of about two to three feet onto a 2 x 2-foot square piece of Plexiglas and then simply picking up the Plexiglas and carefully placing it atop the awaiting soft box. I have since begun a series of broken bottles and jars, and this is but one of the many images I have taken so far. Who knows, maybe I will do a "fine art" book on this subject and call it *Splatter*.

17–55mm lens at 35mm, f/16 for 1/250 sec.

THEMES

Sometimes, exploring a theme through a series of photos helps to reveal your compositional strengths and weaknesses. If your theme involves landscape work, it can help you understand the power of a high or low horizon line placement. If it focuses on flower close-ups, you'll soon realize the value of filling the frame.

Just recently I came across a relatively new Web site for shooters, and my hat goes off to the person who came up with this idea: a monthly scavenger hunt for photographers!

The Web site is http://www.sh1ft.org/26things/. Each month, it posts a list of twenty-six things to photograph, and if nothing else, this monthly list could easily spawn twenty-six individual themes!

The example I've included here is just one possible subject. Another good one would be the four seasons, either focusing on the same subject at different times of the year or varying the subject or exploring just one season in depth. The possibilities are endless.

17–55mm lens at 28mm, f/11 for 1/30 sec.

This past winter at an Old Navy store in New York City, I spotted a bin filled with striped red balls. I don't know why, as is often the case, but I was immediately hit with the idea of buying one of the balls and taking it with me on my travels over the next twelve months, photographing it in a host of locations. Although I've been working on this theme for just a short time, it is clearly one with endless possibilities. Who knows, but maybe someday I will release a book entitled, simply enough, *Having a Ball!*

17–55mm lens at 24mm, f/16 for 1/125 sec.

17–55mm lens at 20mm, f/8 for 1/60 sec.

17–55mm lens at 17mm, f/22 for 1/60 sec.

12–24mm lens at 14mm, f/22 for 1/45 sec.

70–200mm lens at 100mm, f/16 for 1/100 sec.

70–200mm lens at 200mm, f/22 for 1/60 sec.

17–55mm lens at 22mm, f/22 for 1/60 sec.

*12–24mm lens at 16mm,
f/22 for 1/25 sec.*

Full frame fish-eye lens, f/8 for 1/250 sec.

GOOD MACRO SUBJECTS

Macro, or close-up, photography continues to enjoy great popularity, for both amateurs and professionals. While such obvious subjects as flowers, butterflies, and insects are ideal for beautiful close-up images, so are the more unusual subjects: I've noticed more and more that my students are focusing close-up on the abstract and industrial world—and coming away with some truly compelling imagery.

I recall years ago an advertisement selling a guide entitled *A Lazy Man's Way to Riches*, which promised to tell you step by step how to get rich if, of course, you purchased it for $59.95. I never ordered the booklet, so I never did actually discover the lazy man's way to riches, but I can promise you a wealth of photographic riches in the macro arena. Close-up photography truly is the lazy man's way to photographic riches since you can do a lot of your "looking" on your knees and belly—without leaving your house or immediate environs!

Simply grab your camera and macro lens, or a 40–60mm focal length and an extension tube, and start crawling around on the floor or in your yard. As you keep your camera to your eye, you will soon notice the rich textures on that pair of worn out sneakers or on your child's favorite toy. The possibilities are endless.

Opportunities to shoot close-ups are right inside your home, and with a stable tripod, a small table, and a lone window for light, you can spend hours making a multitude of discoveries.

For example, a simple lemon slice can make a bold statement of color and texture when seen and photographed close-up. Note the use of the green wrapping paper in the background. Since depth of field is so shallow when shooting close-ups, I was able to render the leaf pattern of the paper as abstract to emulate green grass—as if to suggest that this image was made outdoors. Additionally, I used sparkling water, not tap water, and with each and every shot (a total of sixteen attempts), I would also add a few dashes of salt to create even more carbonation in the water.

Opposite: 70–180mm Nikkor Micro lens, f/22 for 1/8 sec.

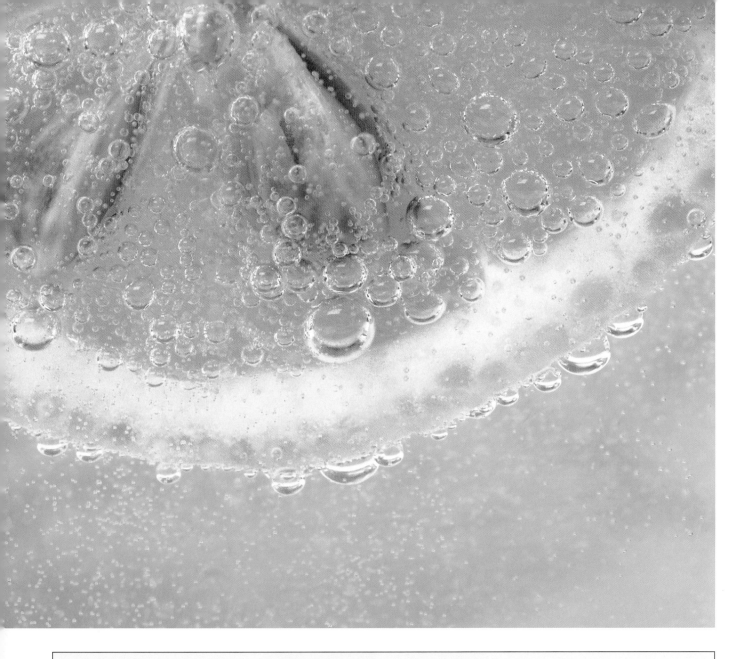

MACRO ACCESSORIES

EXTENSION TUBES

These are hollow metal tubes that fit between the lens and camera body, and are normally sold in sets of three. The combination of the lens and number of tubes used determines the image magnification. Extension tubes are wonderful and welcome accessories for anyone who enjoys photographing butterflies, bees, and grasshoppers. When you combine a telephoto or telephoto zoom with extension tubes, you can shoot these subjects up close without having to be so physically close that you frighten them off.

Most camera manufacturers (for example, Nikon, Canon, Minolta, etc.) make extension tubes for their particular systems, but the favored extension tube brand seems to be Kenko. The Kenko tubes not only let you maintain full exposure control, but they also allow you to use autofocus.

CLOSE-UP FILTERS

Close-up filters are less expensive than extension tubes, but they do tend to produce unsharp images, particularly around the edges.

MACRO DEPTH OF FIELD AND LENSES

Working at such close distances differs greatly from shooting "normal" scenes, particularly when it comes to the 'right' aperture choice. Since depth of field *always* decreases as you focus closer and closer to your subject, the depth of field in macro photography is extremely shallow.

As those who have already explored the world of close-up photography have discovered, the slightest shift in point of view can change the focus point dramatically. Since everything is magnified, even the slightest breeze will test your patience, as what is actually only a five-mph breeze registers as a fifty-mph gust in your viewfinder. Needless to say, critical focusing, a steady pair of elbows, a beanbag, or a tripod are essential in recording exacting sharpness when shooting close-ups.

For those of you shooting with a fixed-lens digital camera, the world of close-up photography opens some exciting doors that are your and yours alone! As I mentioned in my discussion on storytelling apertures, $f/11$ on a fixed-lens digital camera is equivalent to $f/64$ on a 35mm SLR camera. That's one heck of a lot of depth of field at your disposal! And, if truth be told, all of us digital SLR camera users are envious of you and your fixed-lens digital camera for this reason. Oh sure, I do have a macro lens that can go to $f/32$, but to go one stop further to $f/64$, oh that would be so nice. It could make such a difference in much of my close-up work. Granted,

Any number of kitchen gadgets placed on a table and over brightly colored pieces of construction paper or poster board can make great macro subjects. The naturally metallic and reflective surfaces of many of these items pick up the color of the paper, and you'll soon be lost in an abstract world of texture, shape, and color. This image of a simple cheese grater lying on pieces of rose and green paper becomes a piece of art that could adorn your kitchen wall.

(Note: The dings and scratches on the cheese grater are not digital noise but simply the battle scars of a well-used cheese grater that has also seen numerous washings with a scrub brush.)

70–180mm Nikkor Micro lens,
f/11 for 1/30 sec.

shutter speeds are already slow enough when I shoot at $f/32$, but even so, I would patiently wait for the breeze to stop—hours, if necessary—just so that I could call upon $f/64$.

But like I said, $f/64$ is reserved for those shooting with a fixed-lens digital camera. And here's another bit of good fortune. You are able to achieve depth of field equivalent to an aperture opening of $f/64$, but your lens remains at $f/11$. Not only do you get to record some amazing depth of field, but you can do so at relatively fast shutter speeds! If you've ever wanted an excuse to shoot some amazing close-ups, I can

think of no better reason than this bit of news. So, if your camera allows for the use of a close-up filter or close-up lens, you might consider buying it just for this reason.

If you're using a digital SLR camera and a telephoto or macro lens that was designed for a film camera, you have another reason to celebrate the smaller sensor size currently found on most digital SLRs. The focal length of a lens that was intended for a 35mm film camera increases by either a factor of 1.3, 1.4, or 1.6, depending on which digital camera you own. So, when you are making life-size images with a

A NOTE ABOUT LENSES

Most zoom lenses set at the "macro" length are able to offer only a quarter life-size image on film (about half life-size when using a digital SLR camera). Macro lenses are available in various focal lengths: 50mm, 60mm, 90mm, 100mm, 105mm, 200mm, and my favorite of all, the Nikkor 70–180mm.

Nothing can ruin a summer vacation quicker than rain! But, then again, with your macro gear you can still turn it into something memorable. Sitting out on the terrace of my hotel room in Cancun, lamenting the last twenty-four hours of rain, I took notice of the rain-splattered glass railing and framed up the scene of the windswept vacant beach below. I used a tripod and $f/22$ for maximum depth of field, and adjusted my shutter speed to 1/4 sec. for a correct exposure. I chose not to use the Cloudy white balance setting as I wanted to record the overall blue light to emphasize the inclement weather.

Opposite: 35–70mm lens, f/22 for 1/4 sec.

macro lens on a digital SLR camera, the subject is rendered larger than life-size, and again, depending on the camera you own, that may be a 1.3:1, 1.4:1, or 1.6:1 ratio instead of the normal 1:1 life-size ratio. And, when shooting these macro photographs, you still have the same depth of field of the original lens! If you're using the 105mm Nikkor Micro lens, you're gaining focal length: It becomes a 142mm micro lens, *without* losing the depth of field of the 105mm lens.

If you're going to photograph in any of the many different autoexposure modes that are available with today's digital cameras, I would highly recommend that you make Aperture Priority mode your first choice. In this mode, you choose the aperture, and the camera then chooses the correct shutter speed based on both the aperture and the light that is falling on the subject. With current cameras, you can shoot in a semiautomatic mode with hardly a worry about the overall exposure, due to the highly sophisticated and very sensitive metering capabilities that these cameras offer. Plus if you're off a bit, you can always correct it *if you shoot all your work in the raw format.*

In the world of close-up photography, the slightest shift in point of view can change the focus point dramatically.

SPECULAR HIGHLIGHTS

In addition to the very narrow depth of field for which macro work is known, there is also another phenomenon about close-up work that most photographers either don't know about or fail to exploit very often: specular highlights. These are most often seen as out-of-focus hexagonal shapes that show up in either the background or foreground in macro images of subjects that are surrounded by bright highlights. A probable example of a subject that would result in specular highlights would be a single dew-laden blade of grass surrounded by other dew-covered blades of grass all brightly lit up by the early morning sunlight. Dew-covered spiderwebs also work well.

In macro imagery, there's an optical law that goes into effect immediately! Any out-of-focus spot(s) of light will assume the shape of the aperture in use. So, using the grass as an example again, when you focus on that single blade of dew-covered grass in early-morning light, every single other out-of-focus dewdrop that lies within your frame will record as an out-of-focus shape determined by your choice of aperture. If you're at any other aperture other than wide open, you will record hexagonal shapes, because this is the a shape made inside the lens when the aperture is stopped down. At a wide-open aperture, these shapes will record as circles, since a wide open aperture is always a full circle.

With my 70–180mm Nikkor Micro lens, I'm often drawn to subjects as simple as green grass covered in early morning dew, whether it be in my own front yard, a neighbor's garden, or the local park. On this particular day, I found myself on my belly at a local rest stop in Vermont and spent more than an hour lost in the world of specular highlights. I had no trouble finding a subject since everywhere I turned I found another blade of grass "dressed" in a full suit of dew.

Photographing specular highlights is most effective when the dewdrops are backlit (you are facing east). And of course, early morning is the only time when the dew is present, so if you need an excuse to get up at sunrise, this photographic opportunity would be it. Again, the specular highlights here are nothing more than other dewdrops that were nearby but out of the range of focus.

70–180mm Nikkor Micro lens, f/16 for 1/60 sec.

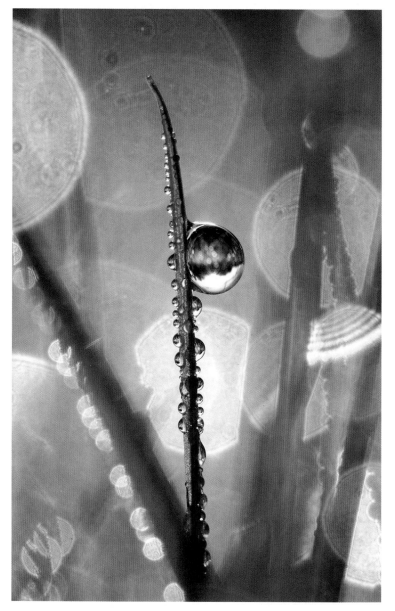

It was also in Vermont, just off a country road, that I caught sight of this field with numerous spiderwebs, all covered in dew. It was just shortly after sunrise and facing east that I placed my camera and 70–180mm Micro Nikkor lens on tripod. I made certain to be as parallel to the web as possible since depth of field is so shallow when shooting close-ups. Then with my aperture set to *f*/22, I simply framed the web as you see it here and adjusted the shutter speed until the meter indicated that 1/30 sec. was a correct exposure.

In this particular instance, I recorded a wonderful rainbow in one of the highlights. This is caused by light refractions, similar to what you see when light shines through a crystal chandelier. Of course there's no chandelier behind this web—only a whole bunch of other out-of-focus dewdrops that simply reflect the shape of my aperture. I just got lucky to be in the right position to record the rainbow (I noticed that if I shifted to the left or right, the rainbow disappeared).

Also, take a look at the specular highlights in both this and the previous image. Did you notice that the size of the highlights varies? This is due to how close or how far each dewdrop is from the plane of focus. The farther the out-of-focus dewdrops are from the plane of focus, the larger and more diffused they will become.

70–180mm Nikkor Micro lens, f/22 for 1/30 sec.

THE PHOTOSHOP
DIGITAL DARKROOM

PHOTOGRAPHY AND PHOTOSHOP: IT'S LIKE DRIVING

Up to this point, all of my emphasis in this book has been on getting the image right in-camera, and with good reason. Taking pictures is a lot like getting behind the wheel of a well-equipped car. Besides the "simple" task of getting behind the wheel, stepping on the gas, and steering the car in the right direction, you must also become familiar with all of the switches, dials, and buttons. Driving a car also requires a keen sense of what's going on around you, but with practice and patience, you soon drive with confidence, by day or night and in all types of weather. Of course, there are those other drivers who jump the curb, run red lights, veer into on coming traffic, and speed constantly. These are the reckless drivers, the ones who keep the auto body shops in business.

Unfortunately, when it comes to digital image-making, many shooters are guilty of shooting with *reckless* abandon—with hardly a care in the world about learning what the camera is doing or where the camera is actually "taking" them. Part of the blame can be placed on the camera manufacturers and camera store salespeople who espouse the ease of taking pictures ("Just push the shutter release and the camera will do *everything* else for you"). But I can't imagine anyone going into a car dealership and believing a salesperson who says, All you have to do is turn the ignition, face the direction you want to go, and the car will see that you get there safely."

Yet a lot of shooters believe it's possible to "just push the shutter release." As a result, many of their images are like a car speeding the wrong way down a one-way street with no one at the wheel. Luckily, the "damage" effects solely the reckless "driver" (the photographer). And since no one else gets hurt by the reckless abandon of these photographers, they are slow to embrace a few of the simple rules about image-making.

In addition to the promise of picture-taking ease made by well-intentioned camera store salespeople and camera manufacturers, Photoshop and other photo-imaging programs are also guilty of perpetuating the myth that any damage can be fixed, no matter how grave. It seems the current mantra— said, with glee I might add, by the amateur photographer—is, "If I fail in-camera I can always fix the problem in Photoshop!" My response to this is, Photoshop *is not* an auto body shop!

Please don't misinterpret me, as I'm a strong believer in the value of Photoshop, but why would you choose to spend time in Photoshop fixing all the damage that you could have easily avoided if you had simply steered your camera in the right direction? What is so hard about choosing the right aperture? What is so hard about using the right lens? What is so hard about paying attention to the time of day? What is so hard about paying attention to the background? What is so hard about placing one foot in front of the other and simply walking closer to your subject? What is so hard about turning the camera vertically when an obvious vertical subject is before you?

The time you invest behind "the wheel of" your camera will be time well spent in learning what your camera and lens can and cannot do—and this is particularly true of the digital SLR camera. How on earth can you *not* help but learn with the instant feedback of that LCD screen on the back your camera? Can't you see that the horizon line is crooked? Good, so shoot another image—*right now*—with the horizon line straight. Can't you see that the background shows the light pole growing out of your child's head? Good, so change your point of view, or have your child move a few feet left or right and shoot another image—*right now*! Can't you see that the exposure is way too "hot"? Good, so adjust your shutter speed a stop or two if you're in manual mode, or adjust your autoexposure overrides to -1 and -2 and shoot two more images *right now*! Can't you see that the lone flower you composed doesn't even come close to filling the frame? Good, either change to a longer focal length or move in closer and shoot another image *right now*! The more "work" you get done in-camera, the more time you'll have to truly "play" in Photoshop.

Having said that, despite your best intentions, some of your images will pick up a "ding" or a "scrape"—even the best "drivers" among us have a lapse in judgment, and this is certainly a reason to call upon Photoshop. But a ding or a scrape is a far cry from a head-on collision, and I want to stress—for the last time, I promise—that you should not think of Photoshop as an auto body shop unless you are in the business of restoring old photographs (those that are really old, faded, and torn).

Photoshop can however, be a valuable tool in customizing your images. In much the same way that an auto body shop can turn an ordinary car into a "custom car," with flared fenders, chrome rims, metallic paint, tucked and rolled leather seats, plush carpeting, and even a musical horn, Photoshop can turn an ordinary image into one that's truly extra-ordinary. And, as I'm sure the mechanics at the auto body shop would agree, it will save a great deal of time if you arrive at the shop with your ordinary car completely intact.

So, although Photoshop is said to offer more than one hundred ways to change or alter your image, I include in this chapter only those techniques that have proved the most fun, valuable, and, subsequently, useful. If you're interested in really learning all there is to know about Photoshop, you won't find that here. But, Photoshop and other photo-imaging programs are here to stay. You will never succeed in digital image-making without these software programs since they are a necessary part of your workflow.

For example, you'll never "process" or print your results without them. Gone are the days of dropping off a roll of film at the photo lab and picking it up two hours later, leaving you with only the simple task of placing the pictures into the family photo album. But the added imaging-program "work" that's now required is, for the most part, fun. I've met many shooters who report that digital photography has become a family affair, with more than just the picture-taker getting into the act. Perhaps the greatest benefit of digital photographic technology has been that tiny monitor on the back of the camera. When photographing family members especially, everyone is quick to take a look at the LCD, and then the race is on to get the pictures uploaded to the computer (for the larger view) and printed in living color or black and white (for all to see).

Although I'm a photographer from the old school (meaning, I still find creating the image in-camera more rewarding than doing it in Photoshop), I have noticed in the past year that I'm finding more reasons to spend time on the computer as I discover another useful tool or shortcut. While Photoshop is, for some, the primary tool for creating images of great emotion and feeling, I've found Photoshop to be no more or less important than a necessary filter or lens—all extend my range of creative image-making possibilities. Now let's go have some fun in Photoshop!

PHOTOSHOP, PHOTOGRAPHIC TRUTH & INTEGRITY

And one final note about the use of Photoshop: Several months ago, one of my students asked my thoughts about ethics in photography and the use of Photoshop. His primary concern was about the truth of the photograph; for example, was that full moon really there when you shot that landscape or did you add it in Photoshop, or was that kid really running from the grizzly bear or was he actually running at the local park but you replaced the background with a charging grizzly bear? My answer may seem surprising since I've probably made it clear throughout this book that I'm a purist at heart and believe in getting the shot right in-camera, but as far as I'm concerned, the real "truth" of any photograph—as in all art—lies in its ability to evoke emotion. I could honestly care less if the image in question was made in-camera or in Photoshop.

Having said that, do I consider the use of Photoshop and the making of composites to be the truth? No. Yet many Photoshop composites have evoked some strong emotional responses from me—but this has been under the umbrella of *knowing* they were composites, and therein lies the difference. If we are *led to believe* that the photographer was very lucky in being at the right place at the right time and then we discover later that the phenomenal sky and rainbow were added in Photoshop, it hurts *everyone* in the industry for obvious reasons. I feel sorry for the truly lucky shooter who really was at the right place at the right time and got that "unbelievable shot," since he or she is now looked upon with suspicion.

If you have added something to, or removed something from, an image in Photoshop, say so. And the same holds true even when you move something in, or add something to, the environment while composing a shot in-camera. Fair enough? That has been my philosophy, and I never hesitate to tell other photographers when any image of mine has been altered.

The more "work" you get done in-camera, the more time you'll have to truly "play" in Photoshop.

OPENING AND CLEANING A DIGITAL FILE

There is a plethora of image-editing software out there, and far be it from me to suggest that all of us use the same make and model. But my familiarity with image-editing software begins and ends with Photoshop, and for that reason, all of my tips and suggestions are based on, and relate to, the Photoshop platform. That doesn't mean, however, that you can't benefit from the information here if you're not using Photoshop, but rather, you will need to investigate what and where the comparable features in your software are and adjust things for the specific nuances of your software.

For those of you who insist on shooting in JPEG FINE mode, and if you haven't done so already, open up each of your keepers and immediately save them as TIFFs by selecting the Save As command and choosing TIFF as the new file extension. Before you do any work on any JPEG file, you should always save it first as a TIFF. Remember that a JPEG is a *lossy* file, meaning it loses data every time it is opened and/or altered; even if all you do is change its position from horizontal to vertical, the JPEG will lose a minute amount of data!

Once you have your folder of keepers, click on the folder to open it and view the thumbnail versions and sizes of the images contained in it. If you click on one of your keepers, it will open up in front of the thumbnails of the other images. Assuming you're working with raw files, this is the stage at which you are given the option of changing your white balance setting (options are: Daylight, Cloudy, Shade, Tungsten, Fluorescent, and Flash). You may notice that when choosing a different white balance, the color temperature indicator also changes; in effect, your white balance setting has a great impact on the overall *temperature* of your image, making it appear either *warm* or *cool*.

In addition to affecting the color temperature with the white balance, you probably have the option of changing the color temperature via a separate control, independent of the white balance, and this is intended for fine-tuning the color temperature.

You also have the ability to change the overall exposure, and you can do this via a slider control or a simple arrow that you click; with each click, you can either increase or decrease your exposure in the highlights or shadows or both. Does this sound like a lot of work? It is, *if you failed to set a correct exposure in camera* or if you insist on shooting in auto white balance. Getting the exposure right in camera saves a great deal of time. And, as I mentioned previously, when the white balance is set to Cloudy, you will find very little reason to change it to something else in postprocessing.

CLEANING IMAGES WITH THE HEALING BRUSH

Perhaps you felt as I did the first time you opened up an image only to discover that it was covered with dust bunnies. I know my lens was clean, and I know my subject wasn't covered in dust, so where the heck did the dust come from?

Welcome to the world of digital, where the world of dust has found a new breeding ground! Digital photography, unlike film, does have one big drawback, and it's this: Most digital SLR image sensors do a great job of recording an image, but they also attract dust like a magnet attracts metal. If there is a single dust speck anywhere near the image sensor, it will be attracted to the sensor.

To avoid dust, first and foremost *don't* change lenses in a dust storm—in fact, don't bother shooting in a dust storm at all! Second, *turn off* the camera every time you change lenses, since the static charge of this simple maneuver will draw dust right onto the sensor.

Despite your good intentions, however, dust will still eventually get in, and when it does, you can follow the manufacturer's advice for getting the sensor cleaned, which in most cases will mean sending it in to an authorized camera repair service. This is certainly an option. Manufacturers say, in effect, that any other attempts to clean the sensor may not only damage the sensor but may also void the warranty. That's a fairly strong warning, and whether you choose to heed it is, of course, up to you.

Whether you send your camera out for cleaning or opt to try my cleaning method (see box, opposite), you might leave the house with your camera free of the dust specks for now, but chances are good that one or several specks will work their way onto the sensor again—and you won't always notice it until after you've downloaded your images onto the computer. Get used to it, at least for the time being, since most of the cameras on the market do not, as of yet, have dustproof sensors. And despite their annoying appearance, these dust bunnies will make it easier to embrace one of the quickest fixes for dust specks that Photoshop CS can offer: the Healing Brush.

Call upon the Healing Brush and, presto!, those dust specks are gone. Since I usually have to open my keepers in some kind of imaging software program to get them "ready," I make it a point to enlarge the images to 100 percent. Using the sliders, or scroll bars, bordering the frame, I go up and down and side to side looking for any dirt spots. It takes but a minute at the most, and it's a simple precautionary measure that makes sense, since most of my work is going out the

HOW I CLEAN MY IMAGE SENSOR

I don't know about you, but I don't relish parting with my camera for a few days just to get it cleaned, so I came up with an easier solution to sensor cleaning. However, I will not take any responsibility for any damage that may result to your camera if you choose to follow my suggestion. In addition to your camera and lens, you'll need a sheet of white paper and a can of compressed air.

1. Put the piece of white paper in a well-lit room, near a window perhaps, and then get your camera and lens ready. Set the aperture to *f*/22 and the ISO to the lowest setting (for example, 100), and take a picture of the paper, focusing as close as you can so that the frame is filled with nothing but the paper. If necessary use your tripod, and for this one tip, shoot in JPEG FINE mode, since that format will load quicker into the computer (see next step).

2. Now load this image into your computer, and increase the magnification of your monitor to 100 percent to see if any pesky black dust specks show up. (If you don't see dust specks, the sensor is clean and you can move on to another section of this book—or keep reading for future reference). Assuming you see dust specks, turn off your camera, take off the lens, then turn the camera back on. Set the camera to manual-exposure mode and the shutter speed to the longest possible time (for example, 8 seconds, 15 seconds, or even 30 seconds, depending on make and model).

3. Set the camera on a table and with the can of compressed air in one hand, get eye level with the camera's internal mirror. With your free hand, fire the shutter release for the longest possible exposure that your camera will allow, and with your other hand, fire several short bursts of air onto the now exposed sensor (it was hiding behind the mirror, which has now flipped up and out of the way since you have started an exposure). Obviously, you'll want to time this so that you're not firing bursts of air into the camera body while the mirror comes back down—if you do, the force of the air could cause your mirror to become misaligned. Also, *do not* shake the can of air at any time, since this could cause it to spit out "liquid air" and once this liquid air gets on the sensor, the Pixel Family is as good as drowned. It can be, devastating if you shake the can while blowing air onto the sensor; the cost of rebuilding the Pixel Family a new house (i.e., replacing the sensor) is not cheap, to say the least.

4. Turn the camera off, replace the lens, turn the camera on again, and take a picture of that white paper one more time, just to check to see if the sensor is really clean.

---

door to a client or off to one of my stock agencies. Knowing my clients' desire for clean images, I don't want to hear from them that I need to clean up my act. If your interest lies in making prints of your work, you would be wise to do the same, since there's nothing more frustrating than printing out an 11 x 14-inch color print only to discover that you have dirt near the outer petal of that yellow daisy.

The Healing Brush is quite simple to use. First, select it from the toolbox (it's the one that looks like a bandage), find a dust-free part of your image that matches the area around the dust spot in both color and tone, and hold down the Option key on a Mac or the Alt key on a PC. (The cursor changes to a crosshair-like symbol when you do this.) Click on that dust-free area to select it as your source. Release the Option/Alt key and the mouse, and move the mouse to those pesky dust specks. Then "paint" over the specks by moving the mouse while clicking down on it, release the mouse, and voilà, your specks are gone. Note that when you do this, two cursors appear on the image: the circular one that you are painting with and the crosslike one indicating the area you selected as your source. Keep an eye on this latter cursor because any elements from the area it moves over may appear where you are "painting."

The Healing Brush tool is different from the Clone Stamp tool (see pages 130–131) in that it also matches the texture, lighting, transparency, and shading of the source area so that the area you are retouching blends in seamlessly with the rest of the image.

Most digital SLR image sensors do a great job of recording an image, but they are also dust magnets.

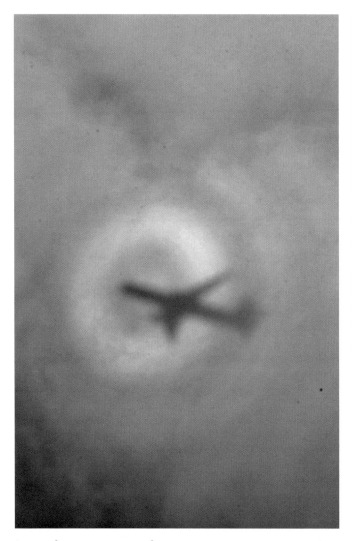

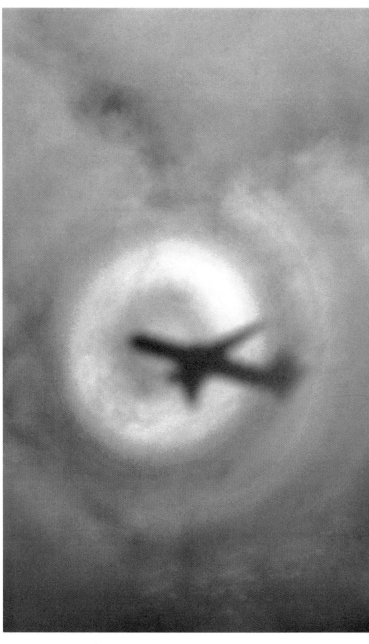

Imagine my surprise when, several days after taking possession of my first-ever digital camera (a Nikon D1X), I uploaded this image onto my computer only to be greeted by dust specks everywhere! I had made this image—one of my first attempts at shooting digital—through the window of a Boeing 777 just prior to descending through low clouds near Paris. The sunlight directly overhead was casting a shadow of the plane onto the low clouds below, and the added bonus of a circular rainbow was too compelling to pass up. I handheld my camera, set an exposure at +1 in Aperture Priority mode to compensate for the bright white clouds (the same thing I do when shooting snow), and proceeded to fire off several frames before the plane was soon immersed in the very clouds.

To clean the dust specks that appeared in the image, I chose a soft-edge brush and a size that was a bit larger than the dust specks themselves. The result is the image at right.

35–70mm lens, f/8 for 1/320 sec.

GETTING THAT "PERFECT" COMPLEXION

I f you find yourself photographing people frequently, and you come across subjects who wish they looked younger or had a better complexion, there's no better tool for the job than the Healing Brush, which can quickly reduce—if not eliminate—signs of aging, poor complexions, or unwanted beauty marks and moles.

What is, perhaps, the one most overused tool in all photo-editing software? The Sharpen tool! I can almost spot an oversharpened image in the dark, since every oversharpened image *glows*—and I do mean it glows! Why does it glow? Let's take a look at the concept of *sharpening*.

First of all, if you're looking to add one more reason to your get-it-right-in-camera list, sharpening should be the first thing you consider. Optical sharpness is—and will always be—about your lens and the quality of your sensor. In theory, the higher-priced lenses and higher megapixel cameras will combine to create the best optical sharpness. But, all digital images require some degree of sharpening, which is where *software sharpness* comes in. This is not to be confused with *optical sharpness*. Normal software sharpening is meant to serve one purpose: to bring out more detail in the sharpness and detail *you have already captured*. You will never be able to *add* detail by sharpening if the detail isn't there to begin with, and therein lies the problem. In an attempt to compensate for a lack of image sharpness (due to camera shake with a slow shutter speed and no tripod or a lack of detailed focusing, for example), photographers will end up oversharpening the image.

Truth be told, sharpening does nothing more than create additional contrast around each pixel, giving *the illusion* that things are sharper. And oversharpening increases the contrast so much that each pixel gets a halo around it—and that's why sharpened images glow. Unless you have plans to help Santa Claus and Rudolph find their way at Christmas with one of your "glowing" prints, make it a point to pay attention to focus and sharpness *in camera*.

If you must do some sharpening, what's the best way to proceed without fear of generating halos? If you're shooting raw and saving to TIFF, or if you're shooting straight to TIFF, the rules are the same: Only after you've made *all* of your adjustments, fine-tuning, layering, color corrections, spotting, cloning, and so on, should you even think about adding some sharpness. Sharpening is *always* the last thing you do.

And note: Most digital cameras offer an in-camera sharpening feature that's tied to the sensor. Every digital image, JPEG or raw, will always record a bit of softness due to the sensor having colored filters laid atop it. That's right, colored filters! Although it's not visible to the human eye, there is a checkerboardlike pattern of red, green, and blue filters on top of the sensor without which the sensor would only record monochromatic color. As film shooters already know, any filter adds a very small amount of softness to the image.

To compensate for this softness, you have the option of turning on the in-camera sharpening feature. In my opinion, you should turn this feature off, assuming you're shooting in raw, since the default setting for in-camera sharpening (a setting you cannot change, by the way) may end up adding more or less sharpening than you want. It makes more sense to have the "freedom" to add any additional sharpness in post-processing. Unless you are shooting JPEGs (basic, normal, or fine), I see no reason to do any sharpening in-camera.

Since JPEG is a compressed file (and a lossy one at that), you should use in-camera sharpening *before* the file gets compressed. Adding sharpness later via the computer means opening the file up once again and losing data.

UNSHARP MASK

Most photo-imaging programs offer sharpening tools, such as Sharpen, Sharpen Edges, Sharpen More, and Unsharp Mask. Only Unsharp Mask offers a choice of how much or how little sharpening to add; the other three choices do it for you within preset parameters—and I have yet to find anyone who knows what those parameters are. This complete control over the amount of sharpness is the biggest reason Unsharp Mask is the favored sharpening choice. (And if you're like me, the name *Unsharp Mask* conjures up anything but a tool that would make an image sharper—just the opposite, in fact; yet it is the sharpening tool that most photographers should use.)

To access Unsharp Mask in Photoshop, choose Sharpen from the Filter pulldown menu. The Unsharp Mask dialog box opens, and you'll see three bars: Amount, Radius, and Threshold. Amount adjusts the intensity of the filter. Radius determines the size of the halo produced around each pixel—and is, thus, the most critical setting of the three. And, Threshold controls the contrast differences between pixels and tells the filter how similar or different the values need to be before putting down the sharpening effect.

Now, here's where it can get tricky, because some photographers want to use one group of settings when they're sharpening just one part of an image, and different settings when they're sharpening up the whole image at once. Sharpening can be a whole chapter unto itself, and this book is not solely about photo-imaging techniques. In fact, I've only scratched the surface, so as someone who has never gone beyond the "norm" in the sharpening arena, I'll just share with you my own personal settings (which I used for all the images in this book and which I use in all of my commercial work): I set Amount at 175 percent, Radius at 2 pixels, and Threshold at 4 levels.

CLONING

Once you've finished cleaning up any dust specks, you can move on to other issues with your image. I'll start with *mergers*. Try as you might, for example, you failed to see that the distant light pole merged with your son's head. The poor kid looks like he has got a real headache, and you would too if you had to walk around all day with a light pole stuck in your head. Mergers are a common problem in photographic composition, more so for the amateur, but even us pros still fall into the trap of becoming so enamored by the subject before us that we fail to see that thing in the background that detracts from the subject itself.

No problem, thanks to the Photoshop Clone Stamp tool. With this tool, you can simply replace or cover that light pole with something else that's nearby, such as blue sky. To do this (in Photoshop CS), you click on the Clone Stamp tool in the toolbox and then hold down the Option key (for Macs) or the Alt key (for PCs). As with the Healing Brush, you'll see the cursor change to a crosshair-like symbol. While still holding down the Option/Alt key, place the cursor over the part of the image you want to use for cloning (in this case, some blue sky) and click on the mouse in that spot. Then release the Option/Alt key. The cursor will change to a small circle. Using the mouse, move that circle to the area you want to cover (in this case, the light pole). Press down on the mouse and use short back-and-forth strokes to go over the light pole, changing it to blue sky. Again, as with the Healing Brush, note that when you do this, two cursors appear on the image: the circular one that's applying the blue sky and a crosslike one over the original blue source area that's being copied (where you initially clicked your crosshair mouse to assign blue sky to it). Keep an eye on the latter cursor because it indicates what area is being cloned over the light pole. If it moves over, say, a bird in the sky, that bird will be cloned where the light pole is, instead of just blue sky being cloned.

It's a really easy fix, as long as the brush size corresponds to the working area. (Brush size can be accessed and adjusted from a pulldown feature on a bar just under the menu bar at the top of the screen.) Too big of a brush size, and just like that, in one sweep, both the light pole *and* your kid will be gone. (That's no problem, though, since Photoshop keeps a history of your actions, and you simply have to go to the history menu, click on the previous step, and the program undoes the mistake—like it never happened. Photoshop also has a Step Backward feature, which continually undoes whatever the last action was.)

Learning how to use the Clone Stamp tool does take practice, not much, but practice nonetheless. And here's bit of a warning: Both the Clone Stamp tool and the Healing Brush tool have become obsessions for many shooters who aspire to perfection. Before they know it, several days have passed while they've sat fixated in front of their computers, forever trying to make every nuance, down to the last pixel, perfect! Knock it off, and go feed the kids!

TIP: VIEW AT 100%—ALL THE TIME

Whenever I'm cleaning up an image using the Healing Brush or removing/adding small details using the Cloning Tool, I make it a point to work on the image at 100 percent magnification. At this level of magnification even the smallest of dust specks and other anomalies can be called out of hiding.

Sometimes, you need to make minor alterations in your digital images, and more often than not, the solution lies in using the Clone Stamp tool, the Healing Brush tool, and the Hue and Saturation controls. I made a total of ten minor changes to this image, taking all of five minutes. Basically, I used the Healing Brush and Clone Stamp tools to remove the distracting small areas of light in the dark shadow areas and also the slight "dings" on the metal pole. In addition, I used the Hue and Saturation controls to change the color in both the sky and the yellow sign, making them a little richer. (To expose this image, I metered off the blue sky in the left of the frame and then recomposed to get the final image.)

12–24mm lens, f/16 for 1/25 sec.

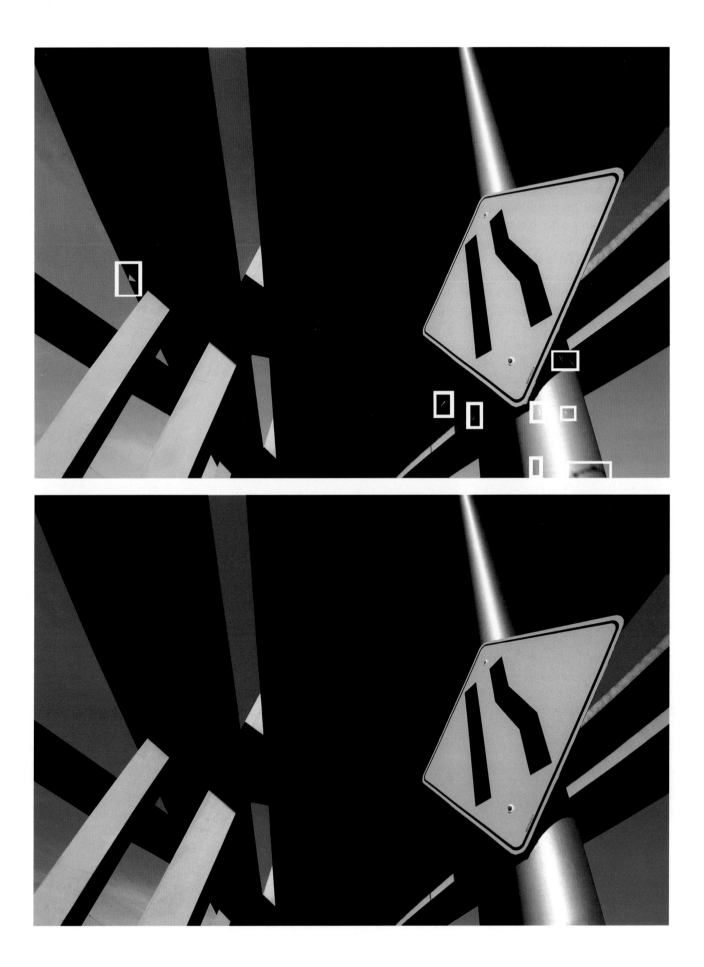

ADJUSTING COLOR

Photoshop offers many options in the arenas of both color and black and white. Sometimes, your digital image needs a simple tweak in its color, while at other times the light when you took the picture was not the light you had hoped for, so you the image needs much more serious tweaking.

I've found that for minor tweaking the Hue/Saturation adjustment controls offer the quickest and most effective solution, but be careful here, since many beginners get really carried away with the level of saturation. Too much saturation looks like too much saturation, and no matter how compelling your composition, it will look, first and foremost, like an image with too much saturation. Keep in mind to make it believable, not unbelievable.

The Hue/Saturation controls are found under Adjustments in the Image pulldown menu. The best way to see which colors you might want to adjust is to open the Hue/Saturation window on your screen and move the slider for Saturation all the way to the right. Make a note of which colors you're seeing where, and then move the slider back to the center (so that the number in the Saturation box reads 0). Now, go into the individual colors in Hue/Saturation in the Edit pulldown menu and adjust them accordingly. Play around with this feature for practice to get the hang of it.

An example of when I might use Hue/Saturation is when I've found myself "burned" by the weather, when my hoped-for low-angled, golden sunset light never materialized due to an incoming storm. I shoot away anyway, as I always do, with the hope of perhaps adding the tone and color of the light that I had been seeking to the photograph later in post-production. For these situations, I call upon the Selective Color adjustment controls, which are also found under Adjustments in the Image pulldown menu (further down beyond Hue/Saturation). They allow me to emphasize (or de-emphasize, as the case may be) specific colors in a scene in much the same way the Hue/Saturation control does—but with even greater latitude.

A word of caution here: You can make the light in any given scene look warm, as if you took the image shortly after sunrise or during that golden hour of light before sunset, *but* if your scene has no shadows, it will look like a cheap rendition of a sunny day.

FILTERS IN PHOTOSHOP CS

Photoshop CS has made it even easier to get those warm colors I love. With the upgrade from Photoshop 7 to Photoshop CS, Adobe added a whole set of adjustments that resemble the filters you'd use on your lenses. And, the best part is that they are available as adjustment layers, so you can apply them to your image and then mask out areas you don't want to be affected by the filter.

So, want to add warmth to an image you took in open shade? On your Photoshop CS menu bar, click on Image, then Adjustments, and then Photo Filter. You'll get a choice of eighteen filters to use on your image, including several that warm things up. You can vary the intensity of these filters; and if you use an Adjustment Layer to add the filter effects, you can apply those filter effects to select parts of your image by using a layer mask. To do this, select any of a number of tools from the toolbox (for example, the Elliptical Marquee tool, the Lasso tool, the Magic Wand tool, and so on), and using the mouse, select an area where you would like to apply a filter effect. The area will be indicated by a dotted line. Then choose Layer on the pulldown menu bar, then New Adjustment Layer, and then Photo Filter. Once the filter list comes up, you can choose your filter for that selected area.

I've found that for minor tweaking the Hue/Saturation adjustment controls offer the quickest and most effective solution.

If there's one constant for every outdoor/nature photographer, it's the ever-changing light and weather. After enjoying clear blue skies and sunshine for the better part of the day, I noticed a large looming storm approaching. It wasn't long before the sun and my hoped-for low-angled, warm light disappeared (left). So, I added, via Photoshop, the color and tones I was unable to record due to the incoming storm. The combination of the Selective Color tool and the Hue/Saturation controls allowed me to come close to getting an image that looked like a scene Mother Nature could have created on her own had the storm not gotten in the way.

200–400mm lens at 300mm, f/22 for 1/90 sec.

BLACK AND WHITE, SEPIA, OR STEELY BLUE

Sometimes, you don't discover that a particular image may have looked better in black and white until you load it into the computer. In Photoshop, this is, once again, not a problem. Although there are many sophisticated Photoshop features you can use (you can buy a comprehensive Photoshop book that details all that), I simply call upon the Desaturate control under Adjustments in the Image pulldown menu, and the color image becomes black and white.

I've told many students over the past three years to create a folder on their computers of twenty or thirty color images and then, just for the fun of it, open each one in Photoshop and apply Desaturate to see what they think. It's another example of the great way that Photoshop can help rescue some possibly ho-hum color shots and reveal them to be real winners when seen in black and white.

And, if you don't want a black-and-white image, but rather an old fashioned, sepia-tone print or a steely blue print, you can do that in Photoshop, as well. After using Desaturate, go to Color Balance (also under Adjustment in the Image pull-down menu) and move the Cyan/Red slider all the way to the right and the Yellow/Blue slider all the way to the left. Just like that, it's a sepia-tone image. Or, move the Cyan/Red slider all the way to the left and the Yellow/Blue slider all the way to the right, and presto, you now have a steely-blue image. Is this fun or what?!

Color Original

The original version of this image was a color slide that I made several years ago on assignment in Ukraine. After scanning the image into the computer using my Nikon Cool Scan 4000, I was quick to see how it might look as a sepia-tone image. As you can see here, it has a feeling that harks back to another era. (I also tried it in black and white and steely blue, as well.) In addition, I made a copy of the image, applied the Gaussian Blur filter to it, and blended the two images together. This accounts for the image's subtle glow.

Black and White

Blue

Sepia

COLOR, BLACK AND WHITE, OR BOTH

So what do you do if you suffer from indecision? Hey, sometimes you take a photograph, and you can't decide if it's better in color or black and white, and rather than make one of each, consider the other alternative: Maybe it's better if it's *both*! In Photoshop, you can have the best of both worlds.

When combining color with black and white, choose one of your iffy color photographs. Next, pick which portion of it you'd like to see in black and white. Now you need to decide if you're going to select either the area you want to keep in color or the area you want to make black and white; choose whichever seems like it would be less difficult to select. To actually select the areas, you can choose from one of several tools from the toolbox: the Lasso tool, the Magic Wand tool (good if the color of the area is fairly uniform), the Pen tool (good if your shape is complex), the Quick Mask Mode, the Paintbrush, or, if you use Photoshop Elements 2.0, the Selection Brush tool.

If using the Lasso tool, very carefully draw a line around the area you want to keep as color. Or, if the area you want to keep in color is a relatively uniform shape, you can also try the Magic Wand tool, which does the same thing as the Lasso tool but will do it for you with a single click of the mouse; but again, the shape must be uniform in tone, color, and contrast, otherwise the Magic Wand won't encompass the whole area. Whatever tool you use, after you select the area with the tool, you'll see those "marching ants" (like a dotted line) encircling it.

At this point, you should tell Photoshop to *feather* your selection, which softens the edges and makes the transition between the selected and unselected areas better. Go to the Select pulldown menu to find Feather, and choose something around 5 pixels for your amount.

If the area that you selected is the part of the photograph that you want to keep in color, go to Select again and choose Inverse. This will surround everything *but* the area of color with those marching ants. Then go to the Image pulldown menu, choose Adjustments, and scroll down to Desaturate. Voilà, you now have both a color and a black-and-white photograph all in one!

While driving through

Arches National Monument last year, I spotted this lone climber from the road, pulled my car over, and immediately set up my camera and tripod. I liked the sense of scale that the lone climber brought to the surrounding cliff face but was not that thrilled with the absence of light (the entire cliff face was in open shade since the sun was off to the left and behind some even larger cliffs). Once I loaded the image into the computer, I used the Lasso tool and "drew" around the edges of the climber. I then chose Inverse from the Select pulldown, and this allowed me to Desaturate the entire image, turning everything except the colorful climber to black and white. Finally, I went to Color Balance (under Adjustments in the Image pulldown menu) and chose 100 percent Cyan and 100 percent Blue with the sliders, and as you can see opposite, that somewhat dull cliff is now transformed into a very cold and steely blue surface. The contrast of blue with the brightly clad, yet small, climber creates a compelling juxtaposition of scale and texture.

80–400mm lens, f/8 for 1/320 sec.

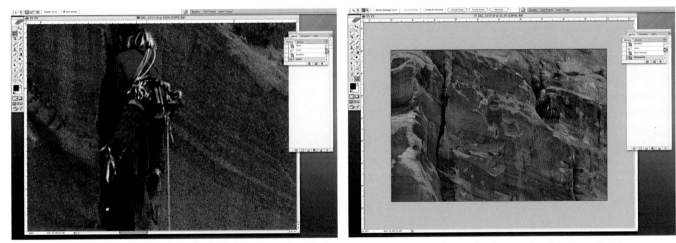

Figure outlined with Lasso tool.

Desaturate turns background to black and white.

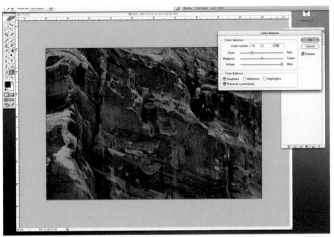

Color Balance adjusts background color.

DIGITAL SANDWICHES

f you're feeling a real hunger for some Photoshop fun, then you'll love something I call a *digital sandwich*. Like this name implies, you start out with multiple images (like two "slices of bread"), but you end up flattening them both and layering them one on top of the other so that they look like one (a sandwich). And you thought only kids have fun! You can use one image and layer it with altered versions of itself, or you can use two or more different images layered together. The simplicity of this technique will have you hooked on making digital sandwiches for months, if not years, to come. Pick any number of your shots, and you'll be amazed at how a ho-hum picture can be transformed into a truly "wow" photograph!

The original version.

Gaussian Blur applied.

When the two are layered together, the result is glowing and ethereal.

SINGLE-IMAGE SANDWICHES: GAUSSIAN BLUR

If I'm using the digital sandwich technique on just one image, I make use of the Gaussian Blur feature. The first thing I do after opening up the image in Photoshop CS is choose Duplicate from the Image pulldown menu. Just like that, I have two identical images side by side. I then choose the Marquee tool from the toolbox, select the rectangular option, and highlight the entire duplicate image with it (the "marching ants" will appear around the entire perimeter of the second image). For the next step, I go to the Gaussian Blur option (from the Filter pulldown menu) and apply a radius of 50 pixels.

After the blur takes effect, I highlight the entire blurred version with the rectangular Marquee tool, go to the Edit pulldown menu, and click on Copy. Then I click on the original image (making it active), return to the Edit pulldown menu, and click on Paste. The blurry image now covers up the original, in-focus one. Then I go to the Layer pulldown menu, go to Layer Style and choose Blending Options. I click on the Blend Modes pulldown options, select Multiply, and, presto!, I now have my sandwich. Finally, I go to the Layer pulldown menu again and scroll down to Flatten Image. These two images have now officially become one, and I am free to make whatever Brightness/Contrast adjustments I feel I may need.

Although flowers are the number one subject for this Gaussian Blur sandwich technique, if you are open to trying it with almost any subject, you will make many new discoveries. A nice landscape in Beaujolais, France, becomes very dreamlike when sandwiched with the blurred version of itself.

80–400mm lens, f/16 for 1/160 sec.

MULTIPLE-IMAGE SANDWICH: NO BLUR

This sandwich technique involves the careful selection of two or more completely different images that, when joined together, can make a new and wonderful single image. You follow the same basic steps as for the single-image sandwich, except you don't use Gaussian Blur and you try other blending modes, including Overlay and Screen, as well as Multiply.

As you get better at this, you'll find yourself paying much closer attention to which subjects work well sandwiched together while you are out photographing. I'm always on the lookout for those awesome blue skies with puffy white clouds—as well as sunsets, sunrises, and moons—that I might use later as part of a digital sandwich. Over a number of years, using both film and now digital, I have amassed a huge collection of these subjects, which I keep in a folder on my desktop and call upon to sandwich with other images that, on their own, fall short of the grade. Although there are many reasons to sandwich images, fixing images with "bad lighting" is my main incentive for sandwiching.

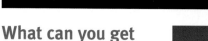

What can you get

when you sandwich a midday overexposed shot of crashing surf along Oregon's coast with an upside-down sunset from Bavaria, Germany? Following the same basic principles for making a sandwich with one image, I was able to create a scene of coastal beauty so real that it fools almost everyone who sees it. I made the original coastal image above with my 80–400mm lens on tripod, and deliberately overexposed it with the idea of combining it with one of the many sunset/sunrise shots in my collection (above right). I also adjusted the color (right), and the result is on the opposite page.

The simplicity of the sandwiching technique will have you hooked on making digital sandwiches for months, if not years, to come.

CREATING YOUR STAPLE OF SANDWICHING IMAGES

If you're like me and have recently become a digital convert, then you no doubt have a plethora of slides or negatives at your disposal. Why not sit down and take the time to see what nuggets of gold are waiting to be mined for use in digital sandwiches?

To get the highest quality scans possible, it's best to scan 35mm slides or negatives with a high-resolution slide scanner. A 50 MB output at 4,000 dpi is the norm, and a scan of this quality will easily produce a high-quality color print of up to 11 x 17 inches, as well as be commercially suitable for stock photography purposes. If you have lots of slides to scan, investing in a good-quality film scanner makes sense. However, there are also some newer flatbed scanners that do just a *decent* job scanning negatives and slides; just don't expect the flatbed scanner to do a *great* job scanning 35mm slides and negatives.

Also keep in mind that your library of potential sandwiching images is not limited to only slide or negative images. There's nothing to prevent you from sandwiching digital images with print film images. Once scanned into the computer, a digital image is a digital image—whether you created with a digital camera or with a scanner.

However, what is important is that any two (or more) images you sandwich be the the same size—otherwise they won't line up correctly, and it often becomes necessary to use noise reduction software on the scan of the slide or negative before you can make the sandwich together with an image shot with a digital camera. Scanned slides and negatives are known for picking up some noise in the scanning process. This is especially true when scanning at very high resolutions, such as 4,000 dpi with a Nikon Cool Scan or 5,000 dpi with Minolta's slide scanner. Both of these scanners offer a Digital Ice feature, and this in one feature that I highly recommend you turn on. It makes for a longer scan time, but it also produces a much cleaner scan. If you would like toe achieve the ultimate in high-quality scans without breaking the bank, check out the downloadable software from the great folks at www.hamrick.com. They even have software available that can turn your scanned slides into raw files!

Since the age of seven, I had always had this idea to take a picture of a group of cowboys on a prairie riding off into the distance, kicking up dust, under the light of a full moon. There was always something comforting to me about a night ride under a full moon, like you would see in *The Lone Ranger*. I didn't learn until twelve years later, shortly after my brother Bill put a camera in my hand, that Hollywood made it look like the Lone Ranger and Tonto were riding at night under a full moon by simply shooting them in black-and-white under a harsh midday sun at severe underexposure. Well thanks to the wonders of Photoshop, I, too, can now create the night ride. And, in my version I've included the full moon!

As soon as I photographed these three real cowboys in eastern Oregon against the somewhat harsh backlight of a mid-afternoon sky, I knew it would make for a great sandwich. With my camera and 200–400mm lens on tripod, I set the aperture to *f*/11, and with the camera in Aperture Priority mode, a somewhat underexposed image resulted. Only a few months ago, and with this book in mind, did I finally add a moon, and I think it's fair to say that it looks real enough.

TIP SHOOT THE MOON—THREE TIMES

Students often ask me how many variations of a sunrise, sunset, moonrise, etc., I make when I see one I like. Much to their surprise, I only shoot *three* variations. Using the Rule of Thirds grid as a guide, I compose three shots: one with the moon or sun in either the lower third of the middle column (A) or the upper third of the middle column (B); one with the moon/sun on either the lower third of the right-hand vertical grid line (C) or the upper third of the right-hand vertical grid line (D); and one with the moon/sun in the middle third of the right column (E).

Again, thanks to Photoshop CS, I can flip or rotate these compositions to "fit" with whatever image I'm using to make my digital sandwich, so there's no need to shoot additional exposures with the moon or sun in other parts of the frame. I'll deal with all the astronomers out there if and when I get complaints about the authenticity of my flipped, or otherwise repositioned, moons. But I am convinced that most of us wouldn't know if the moon were upside down or backward when used as part of a sandwiched image.

Also, I much prefer to shoot the "full moon" the day before it is actually full, since it is still rising and often has a yellow cast, which makes for some wonderful contrast against a dusky blue sky. Note that a yellow moon shot against a dusky blue sky often looks more authentic in a digital sandwich than a moon shot against a black sky. (*Note*: Exposure for a full moon is f/8 for 1/250 sec with ISO 125.)

If you're not able to get a clear shot of the almost-full moon against a dusky blue sky because the moon is not high enough in the sky yet, you can wait a few hours until the moon is higher in the sky. The sky will be black, but you can get an unobstructed view. If you do this, you only need to shoot one composition, but do so at varied focal lengths. Chances are you will be converting all that black sky to white (i.e., transparent) before making a sandwich or composite (see page 144 for more on this); if you don't, all that black will block out the image with which you are sandwiching the moon. Then, once you have isolated the moon, you can simply move it with the Move tool, placing it anywhere you see fit. So, you don't need all the different placements mentioned earlier. Making versions at different focal lengths, however, will give you a selection of moon sizes from which to pick.

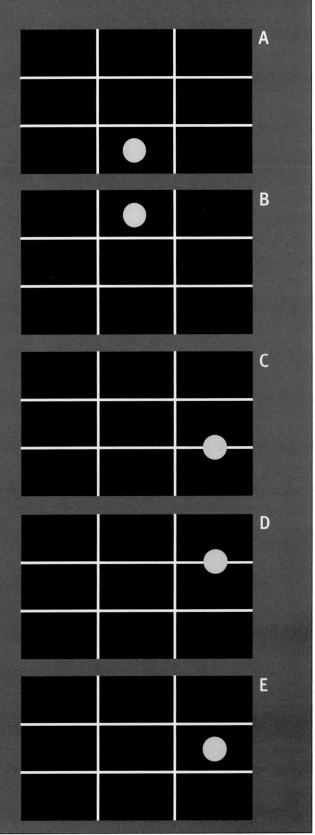

COMPOSITES

Composites are a bit more complex than digital sandwiches, but many of the principles are the same. The chief difference between the two is that a composite normally *requires* that you "erase" (or make white) some things in the original images before the two (or more) photos can be blended effectively. Again, any area of a photo that you make white becomes, in effect, transparent, so when you sandwich that first image with a second image, the second image will show through the white/transparent areas of the first image.

You can achieve this "showing through" of the second image in several ways. For example, you can use the Paste Into feature under the Edit pulldown menu, or you can use the Blending Options under Layer Style in the Layer pulldown menu.

GOING TO WHITE

As previously mentioned briefly, when you are making a sandwich (or a composite) with an image that has dark areas, you may want to make those dark areas white. Any part of an image that is made white is, basically, transparent and will allow parts of other images to show through.

So, how to you change that dark sky around a moon to white, for example, in preparation for sandwiching with a sunset? You could use the Marquee tool. To do this choose the elliptical Marquee tool and use the mouse to drag a circle of "marching ants" around the moon. Use the directional keys to nudge the circle just where you want it. Then go to the Select pulldown menu and choose Inverse. This will highlight the entire background (everything but the moon). Then you simply choose White from the color palette, click on the Paint Bucket, and paint over the dark areas with the white. (If necessary, you can use the Brush tool to make touch-ups so that the white is covering all the black.)

Now, before moving on, go to the Select pulldown menu, and click on Inverse to get the marching ants only around the moon. Choose Select again, go down to Feather, set the Feather Radius to 10 pixels, and hit OK. Feathering softens up the abrupt edge of the moon that is the result of dropping out the sky to white. The image is now ready to be sandwiched.

Perhaps you've found yourself out and about with your camera and are fully aware of that dramatic sky in front of you but are having trouble finding a compelling landscape to go with it. It seems that more often than not, I see some truly incredible skies over lackluster scenes below. Or, I see compelling landscapes under dull gray or plain "perfect" blue skies.

With Photoshop, you no longer have to rely on luck to get both a compelling sky and a compelling landscape at the same time. This is where composites come in. But first, of course, you need to have both a good sky image and good landscape image at your disposal. So, there is a lesson to be learned here: Whether you come across only a great sky or only a great landscape, shoot them both, since you never know when the time will come that you'll want to combine them to form a single image.

For this composite example, my ho-hum image is a wide-angle shot of a barn in the Bavarian hills surrounded by yellow dandelions and an unimpressive sky. I felt it would be just the kind of image that would make a perfect marriage with one of my wide-angle shots of a more dramatic sky. To do this, I first opened up the barn image in Photoshop. I quickly painted all of that lackluster sky white. I then decided that I wanted the dandelions to be "red poppies," and since they are a distant enough element in the image, I could get away with the switch. So, I went to Hue/Saturation under Adjustments in the Image pulldown menu, selected Yellow from the Edit button, and moved the Hue slide to the left until the flowers turned red.

Next, I opened my good sky image, pressed Command + A to get the marching ant highlighting around the entire image, and selected Copy from the Edit pulldown menu. I then returned to the barn image, selected the Marquee tool, and touched the cursor to the white sky area, thereby selecting the sky, which became surrounded with marching ants. Then I chose Paste Into from the Edit pulldown menu, and voilà, all that white sky was replaced by the more dramatic sky. To finish, I used the Move tool to move the new sky around a bit so that the alignment looked as authentic as possible. Once I was satisfied, I selected Flatten Image from the Layer pulldown image. Are we having fun or what?

Barn image with white background

Original sky image

Final composite

PHOTOSHOP AS GRADUATED NEUTRAL-DENSITY FILTER

Graduated neutral-density (GND) filters, which hold back the light over part of your frame, have been used by photographers for more than ten years, and although Photoshop has been around for just a bit less time than that, the concept of using Photoshop to mimic the results of a GND filter didn't seem to occur to anyone until only recently. It makes you wonder what other obvious tools Photoshop has that most of us are too blind to see.

As you know by now, I'm a strong advocate for doing it right in-camera and saving my Photoshop time for more productive things that I just can't do in-camera—such as making color prints. However, there are those times when you walk out of the house without your GND filter, or when you come upon a scene with a horizon line so staggered (mountain peaks, for example) that the "straight line" of the GND filter can't possibly block out all of the strong backlight, or when using the GND filter would end up blocking the exposure of foreground subjects that continue up and beyond the horizon line.

In these situations, the solution is so simple that I'm still amazed that it has only now dawned on photographers! Photoshop has been around since the early '90s!

To use Photoshop as a GND filter, let's imagine you're on a field trip. You come upon a backlit storytelling composition, so you set your aperture to *f*/16 or *f*/22. Take a meter reading

Exposure for ground

Exposure for sky

For the first image (above), I set a correct exposure for the strawberry fields in the foreground, and in so doing, rendered the predawn sky obviously "blown out"—heck, it's basically white. (If this were a color slide, this area would appear almost colorless and transparent on the film.) In the second exposure (above right), I set a correct exposure for the sky, and in doing so, rendered the foreground deeply underexposed, almost black. I then "painted" the underexposed foreground in the second image white, effectively rendering it transparent (right), and sandwiched that version together with the first exposure (the one with the correctly exposed foreground). The result was good exposure overall, much as if I had used a GND filter on my lens (opposite).

Above, left: 17–55mm lens at 28mm, f/22 for 2 seconds
Above, right: 17–55mm lens at 28mm, f/22 for 1/8 sec.

Exposure for sky with ground rendered white

of just the backlit sunrise sky (or sunset sky if you're not a morning person), and adjust your shutter speed until the camera's light meter indicates a correct exposure. Write this exposure down. Next, take a meter reading of the landscape below the sky at the same aperture, again adjust your shutter speed until a correct exposure is indicated, and write this exposure down. Then, if you haven't already done so, put that camera and lens securely on your tripod and compose your shot. You *must* use a tripod for this technique; without one, the image will *never* line up exactly when you put them together in Photoshop. I don't care how steady you might think you are, if you want this to work, you will absolutely need to use a tripod.

Now you're ready to shoot the exposure for *just the sky*. Use the first exposure you wrote down. I'll call this image the backlight image. (Note: This process illustrates just another example of the importance of knowing how to use your camera in manual exposure mode.) Then, shoot your second image at the exposure setting you wrote down for the landscape. I'll call this the landscape image. You're done with part one. Once you get home, load both images into the computer, open both in Photoshop, and follow along with what I did for the examples here. You're basically putting the image together in a way that allows for the correctly exposed parts of each version to appear in the final composite (just as a GND filter renders all parts of a tricky exposure correctly).

Final

MULTIPLE EXPOSURES IN PHOTOSHOP

Recently, Nikon announced its all-new, professional digital camera, the D2X. Of the camera's many new changes (not the least of which is the quantum leap from 5.75 to 12.4 megapixels), I was quick to embrace its ability to record multiple exposures. The advent of the D2X will no doubt push other digital SLR camera manufacturers to include a multiple-exposure feature on their new releases, as well. However, if your current camera doesn't offer this feature—and you don't want to wait until you get a camera that does—you can duplicate the same effect right in Photoshop, albeit over the course of about twenty minutes versus the less than one minute it takes to do it in camera with the Nikon D2X. And, there are a couple of ways to do it, too.

First thing is to head out and find a suitable subject—most any landscape that fills the frame and allows for only a little, if any, sky works the best. Take eight different shots of your scene, varying your composition ever so slightly up or down or side to side. After shooting all eight images, you must create one layer for each in Photoshop and then change the opacity level of each image to 12.5 percent (12.5 x 8 = 100 percent). After you've done all the layers, choose Flatten Image from the Layer pulldown menu and you'll have a multiple exposure.

Your other option is to shoot at an exposure for all eight images as if you had a camera that offered the multiple-exposure feature. It's a simple mathematical calculation that goes like this: Start with the aperture set to $f/16$ and then adjust the shutter speed until a correct exposure is indicated. Let's say at $f/16$ the correct exposure for one image is 1/60 sec. Then if you're sandwiching two images together, you'd need to shoot both images at 1/125 sec. (1/125 + 1/125 = 2/125 or 1/60). So following this, if you're sandwiching four images, each would need to be exposed at 1/250 sec., and if you're sandwiching eight images, each would need 1/500 sec. So, that's the combination you'd use: All eight of your images would be shot at $f/16$ for 1/500 sec. Once again, you would shoot each of these exposures at a slightly different angle, up or down or side to side. Or, you can also shoot each image at a different focal length, in effect zooming the camera with each exposure. (Keep in mind that each single exposures at $f/16$ for 1/500 sec. will be quite dark, so don't be shocked when you download them onto the computer. Also, be forewarned that some digital cameras record noisy exposures when underexposed.)

After you return to the computer, open all eight images and choose one as the Background Layer image. Then, holding the shift key, drag all the other images onto this Background image. Seven new layers will automatically be created atop the background image. Set the blending mode of each layer to Screen (from the Layers palette or under Layer Style⸱⸱⸱⸱›Blending Options⸱⸱⸱⸱›Blend Mode in the Layers pulldown menu) and then choose Flatten Image (again from the Layers pulldown menu). Now you're ready to make any color and contrast adjustments you deem necessary before you print out your image.

Handholding my camera and 17–55mm lens while shooting down into my neighbor's petunia bed would have produced a very ordinary shot. But taking eight exposures, each at different focal lengths, and combining them in Photoshop resulted in a more interesting composition. I know of several photographers who are making a career of producing this kind of "fine art" photography.

CORRECTING KEYSTONING

Keystoning is the term used to describe the "Leaning Tower of Pisa" effect of converging lines in photographs of architectural subjects. It's a very common result when shooting cityscapes with a wide-angle lens. Short of buying a two thousand dollar perspective-control lens, there really isn't any way to avoid these slightly distorted, converging lines. But, within reason, Photoshop can oftentimes straighten those buildings for you, correcting this perspective problem in a matter of seconds.

Open your image in Photoshop, select the Crop tool from the toolbox, and drag the cursor from the top left corner to the bottom right corner and release. You will see the "marching ants" around the entire image. Go to the lower menu bar at the top of the screen and check the small box next to Perspective. Now, using the cursor, drag the top left corner of the marching ant border into the image so that the border is parallel to the tilting structure in the image. Do the same thing on the right side of the image. Then, double click in the image just to the right or left of the small center circle that appears on the image. Photoshop adjusts the image so that any tilting lines appear truly vertical, as they do when the human eye views the actual scene.

"Marching ant" border is dragged inward to run parallel to leaning buildings.

The Lumière Festival

in Lyon, France, takes place every December 8 and lasts for four days. Every single monument, church, and statue of any note is illuminated via a laser show and the church of St. Nezier is no exception. The show starts right at dusk, and with so many monuments lit up at once, it's difficult to photograph several of the displays before the dusky blue sky has turned black. Finding a clear shot is also a challenge as the streets are crawling with photographers, amateurs and professionals alike, so it's best to head out about 45 minutes before the show begins and stake your claim early—of course, with tripod in hand!

12–24mm lens at 20mm, f/16 for 8 seconds

PANORAMAS

What exactly is a panorama photo? It's a composition that extends to the left and right—far beyond the widest reaches of most wide-angle lenses—*without any signs of distortion*. Who doesn't like a great panoramic landscape? I have yet to meet anyone who doesn't. Kodak and Fuji both figured that out, too, so some year ago they introduced their panorama disposal cameras. Although these are not true panorama cameras, they generate a panoramic-like picture format that makes us think they are. In fact, these disposable panoramic cameras are nothing more than cameras with a moderately wide-angle lens and an exposure window designed to crop the normal 35mm film into a panoramic format, cutting off about one quarter of both the top and bottom of the 35mm negative. But what the heck, I liked these cameras enough to have brought several along on a few family outings some years ago. I just couldn't resist the look of those oversized, very long color prints.

But truth be told, to actually go out and shoot a real panorama image, you need to use a true panorama camera—and, of course, a true panorama camera is not cheap. I've owned the Fuji 6X17 Panorama and also the Hasselblad 6X12, both costing several thousands of dollars, and have never been disappointed with the results. For most of us, however, the cost is hard to justify. And until recently, if you wanted to record that sweeping landscape without distortion, your only option was to buy that panorama camera. But now, once again, Photoshop comes to the rescue with its ability to make panoramic images—without the panorama camera itself! It's a technique called *photo-stitching*. (Photoshop doesn't have the corner on this market, by the way; there are many other photo-stitching software programs available, but since my Photoshop CS already includes the photo-stitching feature, I see no reason to buy another program.)

Although panoramas are associated with wide, sweeping visions, don't limit yourself to shooting them with only a wide-angle lens. You can just as easily use a normal or moderate telephoto lens—you'll just have to shoot more exposures. Let me explain the photo-stitching process.

Rule number one when photo-stitching panoramas is the absolute need for a tripod. And, as elementary as this sounds, you will also need to choose a subject worthy of panoramic treatment (although panoramic images often exude strong responses, not everything is deserving of panoramic treatment). When you look out upon a scene before you, establish where your composition will begin and end—not from front to back (as we normally think of things) but from *side to side*. Next, don't tighten down the horizontal

The panoramic format seems the logical choice when shooting any mountain range, since these ranges can seem to go on forever. This shot (from a field above the town of Cordon, France) is a true panorama that I made with my Fuji 6X17 (120mm film format) and 105mm lens on tripod. I used a classic storytelling aperture and set my focus to five feet. The film was Fuji Velvia ISO 50.

105mm lens, f/32 for 1/30 sec.

I used Photoshop's Photomerge feature to combine three separate shots of San Diego into this panoramic image. I metered off the dusky blue sky, then recomposed and shot the three photos, moving from right to left and making certain that the second and third exposures included about a third of the previous frame. I did make a few fine-tuning adjustments (with Levels, Hue/Saturation, and Unsharp Mask) before applying Photomerge to get the final, "stitched-together" panorama. And, although the wait was "long" (five minutes from start to finish) compared to the half a second it would have taken to make this with the Fuji 6X17, I can't help but smile knowing that I didn't spend over two thousand dollars to get it.

17–55mm lens at 45mm, f/11 for 1/2 sec.

Rule number one when photo-stitching panoramas is the absolute need for a tripod.

pivot of your tripod; you'll need to be able to turn the camera freely from side to side.

Rule number two is that the camera be as level as possible. You can buy levels that attach to your camera's hot shoe if you really want to be sure it's level, and you can then test how level it is by first rotating the camera through the entire panorama scene without actually shooting. It also helps if you use manual exposure mode and set the exposure for each image that you intend to use in the stitching process. And finally, it's best to use the same white balance setting throughout the sequence (so, if you have been looking for a reason to follow my suggestion of setting and leaving the WB on Cloudy, this is it).

Once all that's done, begin by taking the first shot of either the far left or far right side of your composition. Then swivel the camera so that the composition now includes about 50 percent of the first composition and 50 percent of new, neighboring subject matter. Repeat this process until you have reached the other end of your panoramic composition.

To make the panorama, open all the images in Photoshop. Open up Levels in the Adjustment Menu, and tweak each one, if needed, so that they are of like value, but don't change the white balance, hue, saturation, cropping, or sharpness. Either save them all to the desktop or put them in a folder. Select Automate from the File pulldown menu, and click on Photomerge. In the window that opens, indicate which images or folder to use, click OK, and in a manner of seconds, Photomerge "stitches" the images together into a panorama. At this point, you can adjust color, contrast, and cropping.

My youngest daughter, Sophie, enjoys posing for the camera, unlike her mother and sister, who often "dread it." She also likes to "act," so it was an easy proposition when I asked her to be part of this panorama idea. The creative possibilities are truly endless if you think of the Photoshop panorama as a movie unfolding. With every frame, you can show another part of your plot as it progresses, and then stitch them together to make an uninterrupted panoramic story.

One possibility, for example, could be to have your subject change outfits from one frame to the next, while the background remains the same throughout. Another idea for the real adventurous (and with the appropriate model, of course) could be to start with a fully clothed model who becomes progressively less clothed and finishes as a nude.

In Sophie's case, she wanted to have fun with different expressions, so we simply planned accordingly.

17–55mm lens at 22mm, 1/60 sec.

Photomerge is in the File pulldown menu under Automate.

Indicate the images or folder of images to use . . .

. . . and Photomerge "stitches" them together.

TIP AVOID SIDELIT SUBJECTS FOR PHOTO-STITCHING

When using Photoshop to stitch together a panorama, you should try to avoid shooting sidelit scenes since most of them often require the use of a polarizing filter. As you move the camera for each shot, the polarizing effect can become either more or less intense in the sky, and this will show up in the overall panorama as a glaring gaffe. As you try out this Photomerge feature, at least in the beginning, shoot only frontlit scenes so that your confidence doesn't get broken in your first few attempts. As you become more familiar with the panorama process, you can take on more challenging subjects and lighting situations—including the ultimate challenge: a backlit sunset sky with a lone tree on the horizon.

CROPPING AND RESIZING

After putting a great deal of thought and technical know-how into creating an image, there's nothing more frustrating than realizing that you still didn't get close enough to fill the frame, or that you didn't see the obvious vertical shot, or that you didn't notice the crooked horizon line. Not a problem, as you discover the ease with which you can crop your image in any number of software imaging programs, Photoshop included. In Photoshop, simply use the Crop tool, and just like that you can cut out distracting stuff on the left and right of your image, or you can crop in really tight to make that vertical composition you wanted, or you can straighten that horizon line.

However, this ease of cropping with software programs is, no doubt, in part behind many photographers' lackadaisical attitude toward getting effective compositions in camera.

These photographers reason, What the heck, I'll just crop it later on the computer.

And there's another downside. Despite how thrilled you might be with the results of your crop on the computer screen, cropping into any image has a price: more noise and a loss of sharpness. And, when you crop out more than 10 to 20 percent, that price becomes more evident.

Let's assume that the original photo was produced with a 6 megapixel camera. The output size of that file—whether it be raw, TIFF, or JPEG FINE—will be around 2048 x 3000 ppi (pixels per inch) or, in more familiar terms, a print size of about 6.8 x 10.2 inches. When you crop 10 to 20 percent of the image, you are in effect casting aside 10 to 20 percent of the pixels. And, assuming you still want to produce an 8 x 10-inch print, you're now requiring that fewer pixels cover the

Here is the classic shot of Mom and the kids on their winter ski vacation (left). It might look familiar if, like so many other shooters, you don't pay attention to what's in your viewfinder. The two *huge* problems? The subjects are too far away and the entire image is crooked. If you wait to correct it in Photoshop, you'll be disappointed. After cropping in closer and straightening, you won't be able to generate a print larger than 5 x 7 inches because you will have cropped out too many pixels. This is why you should slow down and really—and I mean *really*—take a close look at what's going on in the viewfinder before you press the shutter. Ask yourself if things are straight and if you are as close as you can be for the type of composition you want. If, after taking the shot and checking the LCD, you're still not satisfied, try again. It doesn't cost a single penny; the "film" is free, remember?

WEB PREP

When it comes to preparing images for the World Wide Web, there is one rule or standard: Most everything on the Web is in JPEG format. And since you have been convinced to shoot everything in raw format, you may be wondering how to get a JPEG copy of those raw images that you want to send to friends or post to a family or professional Web site. It's actually very easy—and made even easier when you set up an Action in Photoshop.

To create a single JPEG image, simply open up the file, go to Image Size in the Image pulldown menu, set the Resolution to 72 and then in the Pixel Dimensions box you will see Width and Height. If it's a horizontal image, type 700 in the width window. If it's a vertical image, type 700 in the height window. Also, make certain that all three boxes in the bottom of this window—Scale Styles, Constrain Proportions, and Resample Image—are checked. (This should already be done for you since these are checked by default in Photoshop, but maybe the kids found their way to the computer while you were out and. . . .) Now click OK, return to the File pulldown menu, and choose Save As. In the new dialog box that appears, click on Format. Choose JPEG, hit Save, and in the JPEG Options dialog box that opens, set the Quality slider to Maximum and click OK. The image is now ready for the World Wide Web.

To convert a whole batch of images to JPEGs, create an action from the procedure for converting a single image. Then you only have to manually convert the first image in the batch, and all the others that follow will be done automatically. How do you make an Action? First, organize all the images you want to convert to Web-ready JPEGs into one folder. Then, go to Actions in the Window pulldown menu. The Actions palette appears on the right side of your screen. Click on the small icon at the bottom of this palette that looks like a piece of paper with one corner turned up (the Create New Action button). A New Action window opens up and prompts you to name your action; type one in the Name field (for example, Web-Ready Images) and click the Record button (it's the only round one at the bottom).

Now, open the folder that has all the images you want to convert to JPEGs. Once they are all open, you must manually convert the first one using the same steps mentioned for the single-image procedure. As you do this, the Actions palette records every step. After the first one is done, click on the Stop Record button (the square one at far left). You are now ready to Automate all of the other images in that folder. Simply click on the Play Selection button (it's the sideways triangle next to the Record button). When you do this, every image in that folder is automatically converted to the same specifications as the first one; even if you are converting both horizontal and vertical compositions, the same measurement of 700 dpi will be applied to the "long" end (the longer dimension) of the image, whether that is the horizontal or the vertical axis. Pretty cool, huh?

The Actions feature also saves the Actions you create; so when you have a new folder of images you want to convert to Web-ready JPEGs, you can go to the Actions palette and find your previous action (Web-Ready Images, in our example). You merely click on this and the automated process starts up all over again. Nothing could be easier!

---

same 8 x 10-inch area. You're asking the Pixel family to make unreasonable stretches. But stretch they do, and in the end, you will have the results to prove it: Both grain (noise) and a loss of sharpness become evident, and the photograph appears flawed.

There are a number of software programs available to combat these kinds of problems, one of the most popular being Genuine Fractals. This acts as an "instant muscle-building" program. In effect, the remaining Pixel family, all 4,800,000 strong using the previous example, can now pull the same weight of the original 6,000,000 members without so much as a loss in the print quality. But again, this additional software costs money, and then there's the time it takes to do the crop on the computer. Again, just another great reason to strive to make *all* of your compositional arrangements a success in camera!

TIP | DIVIDE BY 200

To figure out the largest print size (in inches) your digital camera can generate while still maintaining the highest quality, divide your camera's vertical and horizontal pixel counts (found in the owner's manual) by 200. For example, the pixel count of my Nikon D2X is 4288 x 2848. So, divided by 200, I get a maximum print size of roughly 21 x 14 inches.

WORKFLOW

So, what are we supposed to do with all of these digital files? I, personally, have no hard and fast rules for managing and storing my images except one: Make backup copies of everything! I was amazed to discover in a recent column written by John Owens at *Popular Photography* and *Digital Magazine* that 74 percent of digital shooters use the computer's internal hard drive to store their images! Yikes! In case you haven't heard, computer hard drives crash, and although not as often, even a Mac will crash. When a hard drive crashes, more often than not, everything is lost.

Here's how I basically operate: My current workhorse for all of my digital workflow is a Mac G5 with dual 1.8 GHz processors, a 250 GB internal hard drive, 2 GBs of RAM, a LaCie 8X external DVD burner, and three LaCie 400 GB external hard drives. In addition, when I'm on the road, I pack my 15.2-inch Macintosh PowerBook with 1.5 GHz processor, 100 GB internal hard drive, 1 GB of RAM, a LaCie 8X external DVD burner, and a LaCie 250 GB external hard drive. Both machines are, of course, loaded with Photoshop CS2.

I shoot *everything* in raw format and always with a 2 GB or 4 GB compact flash card. On average, a one-day commercial shoot will usually generate 8 to 10 GBs of images. In the raw format, that's about 400 to 500 images with my Nikon D2X. Keep in mind that most commercial shoots involve downloading images to the computer several times during the day for on-the-spot viewing by the client. If I'm out on a given day strictly shooting stock photography, I may end up shooting even more images if it's a production shoot (one that involves models) or less if I'm simply shooting "catch as catch can."

Once I've attached the compact flash card to the computer via a USB card reader, I'm able to copy all my images and download them into a folder on the computer's desktop. I give this folder a brief name and always a date, for example Shipyards-Charlotte NC-07-15-04. I then open this same folder via Photoshop CS and can do an even tighter picture edit. I move any images that don't make the grade to the trash, which then leaves me with my keepers, still in their raw state, of course. I then create two sets of color contact sheets of the keepers. Most photo-imaging programs can generate contact sheets, and with most software, including Photoshop CS, the design and layout of the sheets is automated.

To generate a contact sheet with Photoshop, go to Automate in the File pulldown menu and select Contact Sheet II. In the dialog box that comes up, you'll need to indicate the source images (so that the program knows which images to use). So, for Use choose Folder, and then hit the Choose button to highlight the folder with your images (in my example, Shipyards-Charlotte NC-07-15-04). If there are subfolders within your image folder that you want to include, also check the box that reads Include All Subfolders. Then indicate your paper size and print setting in the Document field of the dialog box; I always use 150 dpi, as this gives me both a large and high-quality image size for easy identification when I need to find a particular image. In the Thumbnails field indicate the contact sheet setup. I always choose three columns and four rows, giving me twelve images per 8 x 10-inch contact sheet.

Once my two sets of contact sheets are done, I make three copies of the keepers folder and burn them onto three DVDs, labeling each with the same name as the folder. I use DVDs because they hold considerably more data than CDs; 4.7 GBs versus 700 MBs. One set of contact sheets and one DVD is for the "client" (either an actual commercial client or for my stock agency, Corbis Images). The other contact sheet and two DVDs are for me, and I store them together in my filing cabinets. With both the contact sheets and DVDs completed, I can then move the original image folder to one of two 160 GB external hard drives.

DIGITAL FILE NUMBERS

Every time you insert a compact flash card and take a picture, an image file number is assigned, for example DSC_102, DSC_103, DSC_ 104, and so on. If you don't change the counter to *continuous mode*, you will record these same file numbers over and over every time you insert a card, and if you compile images from several folders, you will get the following message: That file number already exists. Do you want to replace it with the one you are moving? Of course, you don't, since that would literally eliminate an image.

So, if you haven't yet done so, set the counter to *continuous*, and you'll never have to worry about that message coming up again, since every image you take from then on will have its own unique file number. Furthermore, continuous mode will show you how many images you've taken since the day you bought your digital camera, and that could prove invaluable when it comes to justifying your next camera or lens purchase.

INDEX